Mixed-Media

Dollhouses

*techniques and ideas
for doll-size assemblages*

QUARRY

Mixed-Media

Dollhouses

*techniques and ideas
for doll-size assemblages*

BEVERLY MASSACHUSETTS

QUARRY BOOKS

Tally Oliveau and Julie Molina

First published in the United States of America by
Quarry Books, a member of
Quayside Publishing Group
100 Cummings Center
Suite 406-L
Beverly, Massachusetts 01915-6101
Telephone: (978) 282-9590
Fax: (978) 283-2742
www.quarrybooks.com
Visit www.Craftside.Typepad.com for a behind-the-scenes peek at our crafty world!

Library of Congress Cataloging-in-Publication Data
Oliveau, Tally.
  Mixed-media dollhouses : techniques and ideas for doll-size assemblages / Tally Oliveau and Julie Molina.
     p. cm.
  Includes index.
  ISBN-13: 978-1-59253-588-0
  ISBN-10: 1-59253-588-7
  1. Dollhouses. 2. Assemblage (Art) I. Molina, Julie. II. Title.
  TT175.3.O54 2010
  745.592'3--dc22

                                                    2009035364
                                                    CIP

ISBN-13: 978-1-59253-588-0
ISBN-10: 1-59253-588-7

10 9 8 7 6 5 4 3 2 1

Design: John Hall Design Group (www.johnhalldesign.com)
Photography: Ken Chernus Photography
Cover artists: (top to bottom, left to right): Gale Blair (attic), Tally Oliveau (nesting room),
Julie Molina (pondering room), Lisa Myers-Bulmash (bedroom), Debrina Pratt (living room),
Theresa Martin (kitchen), Paula Dion (bathroom)

Printed in Singapore

Contents

Introduction

THE IDEA FOR OUR DOLLHOUSES project was born on a beautiful spring afternoon at the Gypsy Café in Southern California. Julie and I were reminiscing about the dollhouses we'd had as little girls. We recalled the miniature furniture we'd created or saved up to buy at the local dollhouse shop. We described the wallpaper we hung, the beds we made, the windows we embellished, the dolls we sewed dresses for. It was sad that our beloved houses were long gone. How could we have tossed them aside so easily? Oh yeah. We were teenagers.

Artist: Julie Molina

Within the span of that short lunch hour, though, we went from reminiscing to planning. Who was to say we couldn't create our own dollhouses today? Not only could we create them, we could incorporate our artistic selves and even our artistic friends in an altered art assemblage project that had never been done before.

And so the Mixed-Media Dollhouses project was born. The artists in this project created seven houses, each with a different theme: the Tree House, the Under the Sea House, the Gothic House, the Wonderland House, the Circus House, the Castle, and the Hotel Penthouse. Each artist created a different room in each house. Although the houses all include some standard rooms, such as bedrooms, kitchens, dining rooms, and living rooms, each house also incorporates at least two "artistic-license" rooms. These rooms—the Moon Room in the Gothic House, the Pondering Room in the Tree House, and the Aviary in the Castle, for example—turned out to be a lot of fun to create. The *pièces de résistance* of each house, however, were the attics. These were designed to be exceptionally large, to house each artist's fantastical imagining of what was happening there, in keeping with the theme of the house.

If you've picked up this book, you probably have an interest in assemblage art and might even have thought about building your own dollhouse. In the following pages, you'll find plenty of tips and techniques for creating your own assemblage pieces, whether or not they are dollhouses. You'll also find plenty of inspiration in the dollhouses created by the talented artists who participated in our collaborative project. We hope this book will open your heart and mind to the very expressive art of assemblage, in which collage, dollmaking, sewing, paper arts, wire wrapping, and more combine to create a three-dimensional piece of art.

—Tally Oliveau

Opening the Dollhouse Door: Project Background

We chose the dollhouse concept to bring our assemblages to life because dollhouses were close to our hearts, but we wanted to execute the houses with adult ideas and skill. To initiate a larger collaborative project, we asked our many wonderful and talented artist friends to join the fun. Each artist was handpicked for her assemblage experience—or inexperience! We wanted our project to include artists with different levels of skill and with varying styles and sensibilities—each had something unique to contribute and we wanted each artist's muse to guide her through the project using her own point of view. Although each artist's voice shines in her own individual room, the collection came together beautifully in an eclectic but cohesive unit. Our only requirement was that each room be constructed from an altered cigar box.

Because our participating artists were located all over the United States, we assembled an online Yahoo group for the project. The online group allowed everyone to communicate easily; it also provided a forum, so that everyone could be heard and communications didn't need to be repeated and forwarded. Throughout the project, we tracked our progress on the Yahoo group through messages and photos. As a group, we brainstormed and voted on the themes and types of rooms for the houses. Seven themes won the vote: gothic, under the sea, castle, tree house, hotel, circus, and wonderland. The most cerebral—the wonderland theme—was designed to be a combination of a psychedelia, *Alice in Wonderland*, and *Charlie and the Chocolate Factory.*

Once the house themes were in place, we organized an electronic signup sheet for the rooms, each artist choosing one room in each house from the following list: attic, bedroom (2), living room, kitchen or dining room, and two artistic-interpretation rooms. To keep the process fair, we opened up all the rooms in all the houses at the same time. This worked well: most of us got our first choice, because that was the room we signed up for first.

Next, we planned the basic house configurations, so that each artist knew where her rooms were located. Where were the outside walls? Was the room on an upper floor or at the bottom? This helped the artists plan their window and door cutouts and the exterior embellishments. The shapes of the houses were also important. We wanted the Tree House to be tall and straight, like a tree. The Castle was to be wide, with a multilevel rooftop, similar to a real castle. Each house had its own unique silhouette.

Every month, each artist completed one room within the theme of her choice. As the rooms were completed, their work was posted on our Yahoo group site and then mailed to Julie, who acted as our centralized collection point. Roughly nine months later, our project was essentially complete. It was then that we were able to meet and put all the rooms together into a cohesive house. It was exciting to see everyone's work come together!

PAPER GLAZE ADHESIVE

GEL MEDIUM

THICK TACKY GLUE

1 On Your Mark, Get Set, Play!

No doubt you've looked at the lovely dollhouses for sale at craft stores and hobby shops but have put off buying one. Building your own dollhouse, even from a kit, can be daunting: all those little pieces—and that price tag! Creating the dollhouse of your dreams can be fun, but it can also involve a lot of time, patience, and money. And where will you put your great big dollhouse when it's finished?

Prefabricated right down to the furniture, predesigned dollhouses can also be a bit impersonal and, well, boring. As an artist, you want a dollhouse that's more like a work of art and says something about who you are—a dollhouse that breaks the mold and is completely unique.

Maybe you aren't as interested in making a dollhouse as you are in creating assemblage art. Fortunately, the foundation for creating both is the same. This chapter will help you take those first steps toward creating the dollhouse or assemblage piece you want. You'll also find a list of tools and materials needed to decorate and furnish your altered dollhouse.

easy to cut apart,
reconfigure, add on

CIGAR BOXES MAKE GREAT ROOMS.

round boxes
can also be used

sturdy
construction

12

Choosing a Theme

ONE OF THE FIRST STEPS in creating your assemblage, as in any art piece, is choosing a theme or idea to present. If you're not sure where to start, begin with what you love. A jumping-off point might be a favorite novel, song, movie, historical time period, or geographic location. For example, if your favorite movie is "The Wizard of Oz," you might re-create scenes from the movie or dedicate an assemblage to the personality of one or each of the main characters. You might also base your theme on a memory, or a fantasy, of a dream-vacation destination—or even a place on another planet.

Listening to music and flipping through your favorite magazines are more sources of inspiration. What images or emotions does the music evoke? Create a three-dimensional representation of those feelings. Fashion magazines and home décor catalogs are great sources for your own paper dolls and "furniture." A photo in a fashion magazine might be your inspiration for a paper doll. Using the doll as your starting focal point, you can create a world for that paper doll within your assemblage. Start with what your paper doll is wearing, or what you would like it to wear, and then extend your imagination to create the world she or he might inhabit.

If you're new to assemblage, try starting with a photo or image of a loved one, such as your children, spouse, parents, pets, or other family members. Using a familiar image as a focal point for your art piece allows you to feel comfortable within an art form that's new to you. Make multiple copies of the image and print them in multiple sizes. Making several copies gives you "permission" to make mistakes—if you goof up, you can just start over with a fresh copy.

Thinking Inside the Box: Choosing a Substructure

THE FUNDAMENTAL ELEMENT of any dollhouse or assemblage is the structure. Boxes or frames work well for the rooms in your house and for the main structure of your assemblage. Options include cigar boxes in various sizes, shoe boxes, photo collection boxes, box frames, and triangular frames. Smaller options for miniature assemblages include candy and mint

tins and even metal jar tops. We avoided dictating a particular box size for our project, because we wanted the houses to have an organic, asymmetrical look. We were interested in building a dollhouse with a lot of character, with fun eaves and angles that jutted out in strange and interesting ways. If you want your dollhouse to have a more uniform look, be sure to collect boxes of the same size and depth.

For a basic assemblage, you will likely only need light, paper-covered wood boxes. These work well if you're planning to incorporate a lot of cutouts or to drill holes through the sides. If you want to use heavy or large objects in your assemblage, you'll need a box with more stability, so choose a sturdier box frame. Fancy boxes with nice finishes and latches aren't necessary for most projects.

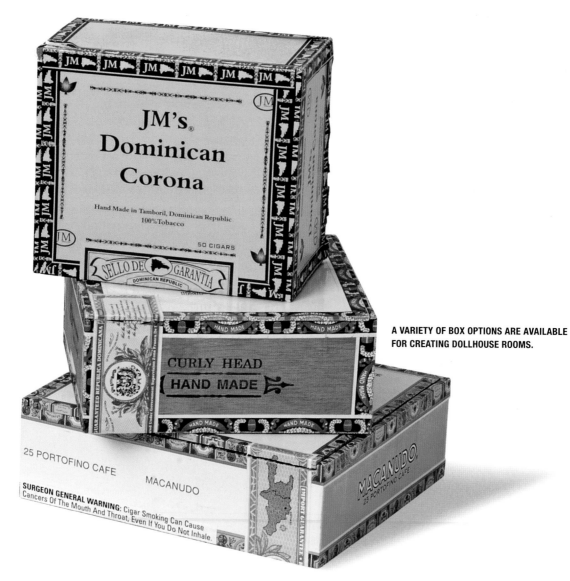

A VARIETY OF BOX OPTIONS ARE AVAILABLE FOR CREATING DOLLHOUSE ROOMS.

Cigar Boxes

Cigar boxes work well for assemblage; they're easy to find, inexpensive, and come in a variety of shapes and sizes. Flea markets and eBay are good sources for cigar boxes in good condition, but the boxes can be overpriced. Your best bet is to visit your local smoke shop, where, if you're lucky, you can get them for free or for a small charge. Call before you drop in, to find out if boxes are available and how much they cost. Tag sales/garage sales are also great places to find these boxes.

Shoe Boxes

Shoe boxes can be a little flimsy, but if you can find sturdy boxes and don't plan on stacking them too high or weighing them down with heavy interiors, they can substitute nicely for cigar boxes. They also tend to be larger and deeper, so there's more room to play.

Photo Collection Boxes

Photo collection boxes are commonly available at craft and art stores and from mass retailers. Sturdier than regular shoe boxes, photo boxes come in a number of different shapes and are made from a variety of materials, including reinforced cardboard and thick wood; these are ideal for housing assemblages with large or heavy pieces. Photo boxes usually come with a lid, which can be removed and used as housing for another assemblage or cut up and used for parts. Some also include a glass front-piece. The glass can be removed, if you prefer an open assemblage, or replaced when your artwork is complete to protect it from dust and prying fingers.

Box Frames

If you're into luxury, this option is for you. Box frames, which can be found at most frame and craft stores, are sturdy, provide a protective glass case for your work, and can be hung on the wall in a formation for a stunning effect. Box frames are available in a number of ready-made shapes, including triangular (originally made for keeping folded flags), which are handy for creating "attics." There are a few drawbacks to using box frames, however: they are expensive, heavy, and fragile. They are also difficult to cut, which means your artistry can be limited if you're not a whiz with power tools.

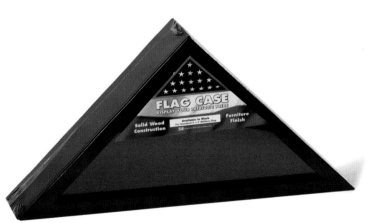

Hunting and Gathering: Assembling Your Supplies

ONCE YOU HAVE COLLECTED your boxes or other assemblage enclosures, you'll want to gather together a few tools and other supplies before you begin creating your dollhouse.

CLOCKWISE: FROM TOP: DREMEL ROTARY TOOL AND ATTACHMENTS, JIGSAW, COPING SAW, CRAFT KNIFE, AWL, AND SANDPAPER

Tools

Power tools can be useful, but you should feel comfortable handling them. Follow the manufacturer's instructions, including safety precautions, when using power tools. Consider practicing with them before beginning a project.

Jigsaw a small power saw that works well for cutting curves and for general cutting in small projects.

Rotary tool an all-purpose power tool with attachments that cut, sand, and drill, such as a Dremel.

Coping saw a manual saw, which is useful for cutting small openings, such as windows and doors, from your boxes. Coping saws usually come with fine-toothed blades for making delicate, smooth cuts.

Awl a needle-like tool for poking holes through lightweight materials, such as paper, chipboard, and even very light wood.

Other Supplies

- Pencil and eraser
- Felt pens
- Ruler
- Scissors and paper cutter
- Craft or other paints in various colors
- Paintbrushes (cheap ones are fine)
- Decorative papers
- Mat board
- Brayer
- Bone folder for smoothing papers
- Chain-nose and round-nose pliers
- Wire cutters
- 18–22-gauge wire in various colors
- Dowels of different sizes, for coiling
- Sandpaper
- Adhesives
- Paper-doll and clip-art books
- All the wonderful goodies you've accumulated over the years at flea markets, tag sales, and estate sales and found objects that you've been saving for that special project. Use them now—this *is* that special project!

Deconstruction and Surface Preparation

REMOVING PAPER FROM CIGAR BOX

Cigar Boxes

The most common type of cigar box is made of thin wood, is covered in paper, and has a lid, which is held on with only a bit of paper border. If you're planning to include the lid in your assemblage, consider reinforcing the paper hinge with another layer of paper, linen tape (usually found with bookmaking supplies), or even a decorative metal hinge. If you don't plan on using the lid, you can easily remove it.

Be sure to save the lids and the interior wooden dividers that are sometimes included in the cigar boxes. These extra pieces can be used as additional walls, doors, and other portions of your assemblage. A real bonus is that they are already perfectly sized to fit on or inside your box. Additionally, they can be used instead of expensive canvas as a foundation for future paintings.

Preparing the Box
To remove the lid, slice along the paper join with a craft knife and separate the parts. Then remove the paper from the box. You'll find that most of the paper from inside the box comes out easily, and the thin, decorative paper border peels away, usually in one long strip. The rest is pretty stuck down, but you have a few options for dealing with it—you can paint or paper over the remaining paper, leave it as is for a funky, vintage look, or sand the original paper off.

CUTTING THE LID OFF A CIGAR BOX WITH A CRAFT KNIFE

Other Boxes

Sturdier cigar or other wood boxes can require more preparation, depending on their condition and your assemblage plans. Use sandpaper or a rotary tool with the sanding attachment to remove layers of unwanted paper or paint. A layer of paint primer or decorative paper can also cover unwanted designs and textures on your box.

Creating Unique Shapes

SOMETIMES A SIMPLE RECTANGLE or square shape just won't do, and you need a more-complex or specific shape to help relate the story in your assemblage. Maybe you're looking for sloped rooftops and angled rooms or to create additional space in some rooms.

You can alter your encasement in a number of ways: by extending the original box to make it larger; by creating unusually shaped encasements or divided spaces using mat board and additional wooden pieces; or, if you find that your artwork simply demands more room, by putting together multiple boxes.

To alter the box, rather than removing the sides, which can compromise its sturdiness, attach additional pieces to the box. These additional pieces can come from a few sources. One option is to use the internal wooden dividers from your cigar box. If the box has no dividers, take apart a similarly sized cigar box and use its sides to create the sloped edges of a roof or additional "walls." Another option is to use mat board, which is easier than wood to cut into any size and shape you need. Cutting mat board requires only a craft knife and a ruler to make clean, straight cuts, or a craft knife and curved ruler or a steady hand for clean, curvy cuts.

Creating a Triangular-shaped Addition

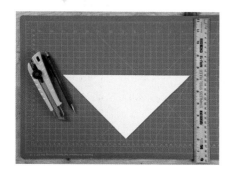

1 **Cut a triangular piece of mat board** to the shape and size of the room you want to add to your box. This piece will become the back of the room.

2 **Cut two pieces of mat board** to the same depth as your box and to the desired length.

3 **Assemble your room addition** using adhesive. Allow to dry completely.

4 **Adhere your completed room addition** to your original assemblage box.

Expanding Your Room

To create a larger box, you can join two or more boxes of the same size together with a new mat-board back piece, cut to the size you need. Using mat board to join the boxes helps to maintain most of the sturdy structure of your original boxes. Be sure to adhere your new pieces well, so you can drill through a wall or add heavy embellishments as you build your assemblage. If your pieces are not adhered well, the walls can fall apart under the pressure of drilling or under the weight of your assemblage elements.

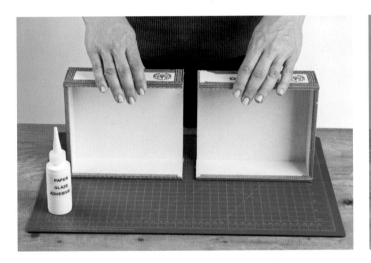
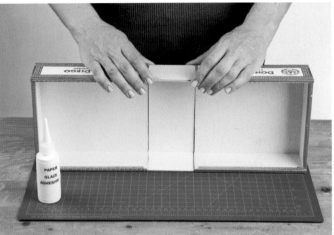

1 **Using two boxes of the same height and depth,** remove one side of each box, so that when the two boxes are placed side by side, the open ends meet. An easy way to remove the side of a cigar box is to gently tap it with a small hammer from the inside of the box; this releases the metal staples. You can also use your chain-nose pliers to pry out the metal staples.

Decide on the desired width of your assemblage encasement. If the width of the two boxes placed together meets your needs, simply connect them on the inside and outside with strong tape. You can also completely remove the back pieces of the two boxes and replace them with one piece of mat board cut to the width of the two boxes put together.

2 **To make an even wider encasement** for your assemblage, cut a piece of mat board that is the same height as your boxes and wide enough to create the additional width you need. The mat board serves as your filler piece and is placed between the two boxes. Use the assemblage box to trace the basic size onto your mat board, remembering that you need to fit the mat board into the *inside* of your box, not the outside. Cut the piece using a craft knife and affix it to the inside of the box with strong tape.

An alternative is to cut a piece of mat board the desired length and replace the original box back with the mat board, as described in Step 1. Adhering the mat board to the inside of the boxes creates an even background surface and additional support for your assemblage. The width of your new box is determined by the size of your background mat board. If there are gaps between your mat board and the back of the original box, fill in those spaces with additional mat board.

Tip You can also take apart a square box and cut the bottom/back piece in half diagonally using a rotary tool or saw. This automatically gives you two triangular pieces to work with!

Creating Unique Shapes

THE HOTEL PENTHOUSE PATIO

Artist: Theresa Martin

Hotel Penthouse Boxes in three sizes were adhered together to create multiple rooms for the Hotel penthouse. The top of the largest box is used as a "patio." The wall behind the patio is cardstock, cut to size. Although this addition looks complex, it is easy to make and adds to the room's character.

Wonderland House Attic For the Wonderland House attic, we removed a side piece from two cigar boxes and joined the boxes with mat board. The angled roof was created using mat board, as well. Molding was used between the upper and lower portions of the assemblage to hide messy connections.

Circus-House Attic For the circus-house attic, we put together several cigar box pieces to create an unusual and effective asymmetrical room. The assemblage remains sturdy because it is attached to one piece of mat board, cut to size and adhered to the back of the assemblage.

Under the Sea House Attic To create the roof for the Under the Sea House, we joined pieces cut from a wooden photo box. Because the sloped roof doesn't extend all the way to the edges of the box beneath, we had room to add embellishments.

THE ANGLED ROOF OF
THE WONDERLAND HOUSE ATTIC

Artist: Tally Oliveau

THE ASYMMETRICAL CIRCUS-HOUSE

Artist: Theresa Martin

THE SLOPED ROOF OF
THE UNDER THE SEA HOUSE ATTIC

Artist: Julie Molina

2 Cut It Out!

You've found the perfect encasement

for your assemblage, you've chosen a terrific theme, and you've gathered together the materials you'll need. You are ready to begin construction!

One of the most attention-grabbing ways to add interest to your assemblage is to include cutouts. Features such as doors, windows, and cutout silhouettes add dimension and can give your rooms a realistic look and feel. Cutouts also add light to your piece by opening up the space. For inspiration, check out the moldings and decorations of windows, doors, and archways you admire in magazines, at home improvement stores, on your travels, and around your neighborhood and town. It's easy to add architectural features to your own assemblage using basic materials.

There are three options for creating cutout features: cutting a hole in your box, which entails using power tools; cutting features from mat board using a craft knife; and creating faux cutout features using rubber-stamp images, paper, moldings, purchased windows and doors, and photos.

Tip Plan ahead! Cut features from the boxes before you assemble your rooms.

Using Tools for Cutting Openings

A cut out was made in the back of the box to give the airy feeling of a tree.

A working door!

A trap door was cut out of the side of the box.

Artist: Lisa Myers-Bulmash

CUTTING OPENINGS IS NOT DIFFICULT if you use boxes made from thin wood, such as cigar boxes. The thin wood is easy to cut and sand. Sturdier wood boxes can be cut if you are skilled with power tools.

When using power tools, be sure to wear safety glasses. Go slowly, watch your fingers, and follow the instructions and precautions that come with the tools. It's a good idea to place a scrap piece of wood under the material you're cutting, so that if you cut through the piece, you won't damage your work surface. In a similar vein, use a self-healing cutting mat when using a craft knife.

Creating a Cutout

1 **Create an outline for the cutout,** by using a pencil, and ruler if needed, to draw the cutting line. For this example, we are cutting a rectangular window from the back of a small cigar box.

2 **Using a rotary tool** with the drill attachment, drill a pilot hole into the cut line, to create a starting place for sawing. In our example, the drill is inserted at a corner of the rectangle, but you can start anywhere, especially if your cutout is curved and has no corners. Using a drill bit with the same dimension as the saw blade makes it easier to insert your saw into the pilot hole.

3 **Insert the blade of a coping saw or jigsaw** into the pilot hole and slowly saw along the pencil lines. When you have cut out the unwanted portions of wood, smooth the remaining edges by sanding them with a piece of fine-grade sandpaper or a rotary tool with the sanding bit attached. Sanding will also remove leftover pencil lines. If you have left exuberant sawing marks or accidental cuts, fill them in with spackle. Save the cut pieces; you can use them to make shutters or other features in your assemblage.

Tip Make it even easier! If you don't feel completely confident about handling the saw but really want to use it, use the rotary tool to first make pilot holes, approximately 1" (2.5 cm) apart, along your pencil lines. This creates a "dotted line," along which you can cut.

Cutouts

Artist: Julie Molina

CASTLE DINING ROOM WINDOWS

Castle Dining Room For the arched windows in the Castle dining room, stained-glass window images from a copyright-free clip art book (published by Dover) were printed onto vellum, cut out, and adhered over the window cutouts with dimensional adhesive. Be sure to cut the vellum at least 1" (2.5 cm) larger all around than your window cutout, to provide enough surface area to glue the vellum onto the box. The stained-glass design adds artistic expression, and the vellum allows a beautiful glow of light to shine through the windows. Purple paper window frames not only mask uneven edges and glue lines but add a realistic and interesting dimension to the walls.

Gothic House Attic To fill the Gothic House attic-window cutouts, stained-glass windows were printed onto clear acetate, cut out, and attached to the box with dimensional adhesive. The neatly cut edges of the wallpaper (decorative paper) cover the joins between the printed acetate window and the assemblage.

Artist: Lisa Myers-Bulmash

GOTHIC HOUSE ATTIC STAINED-GLASS WINDOWS

Gothic House Gypsy Den

The back window of the Gothic House Gypsy Den is trimmed with a purchased paper window frame and a small wooden piece used as a window ledge. The artist also added clever details, such as a pair of store-bought candlesticks and wind chimes created from earring charms and beads. You can almost hear them ringing in the breeze!

On the opposite wall, the cut edges of the side window are masked by copper tape, and the window is trimmed with a frame cut from decorative paper. A little metal-charm bird has perched there.

Artist: Lisa Myers-Bulmash

TREE HOUSE ROOM DOOR

Artist: Julie Molina

GOTHIC HOUSE GYPSY DEN SIDE WINDOW

Artist: Julie Molina

Tree House Room

The working door in the Tree House Room was created by first cutting out a doorway in the side wall of the box. The door was spackled and painted and then reattached to the side wall using miniature hinges. A small door handle, created from a small painted bead, was adhered to the door with tacky glue.

GOTHIC HOUSE GYPSY DEN BACK WINDOW

Craft Knife Method for Cutting Openings

Artist: Tally Oliveau

THE ORIGINAL BOX BACK OF THE TREE HOUSE NESTING ROOM WAS REPLACED BY A PIECE OF MAT BOARD WITH A CUTOUT, TO CREATE A TREE-BRANCH BACKGROUND.

IF YOU'RE UNCOMFORTABLE using power tools, or just want a less-cumbersome approach to creating cutouts, you can cut shapes, such as doors, archways, and furniture, from mat board. Mat board is easy to cut with a craft knife and can also be used to make room separations.

Cutting mat board can sometimes leave rough edges. The best way to avoid rough edges is to use a very sharp blade every time you cut, and to replace your blades often. If you still have a rough edge, you can't sand mat board, but spackle works nicely to cover a multitude of sins. You can also disguise minor cutting deficiencies by covering your mat board pieces with paint and paper as you put together your assemblage.

Creating a Background Cutout

If you plan to remove the box back and replace it with a cutout background, it's important to plan your background carefully. Once the back of the box is removed, you might find that the sides are no longer rigid and the box is flimsy. To retain a fully stable box structure, be sure to extend the background to at least three sides of the frame and avoid cutting out too much of the mat. In the Tree House Nesting Room, for example, the tree branches extend to the other end of the box.

1 **Remove the back of the box** you want to use for the assemblage.

2 **Trace the outline of the removed box** back onto a piece of mat board, then cut along the lines.

3 **Using a pencil,** draw the cutout design on the mat board background piece.

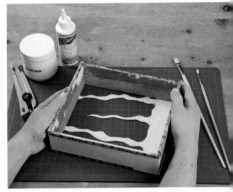

4 **When you are happy with your design,** use a craft knife with a sharp, new blade to cut out the unwanted areas. Use a cork-backed metal ruler as a guide for your craft knife when cutting straight lines. As you become more experienced with your craft knife, you will also feel more comfortable cutting curves and corners. If you have never used a craft knife, practice cutting on scrap mat board pieces before beginning your assemblage piece.

5 **Adhere the background** piece to the box.

Tip By lining up two edges of the box back to two of the outer edges of your mat board, you can make fewer cuts. Use your moldings and stamped window-frame images as templates for your cutouts.

Mat Board Cutouts

Artist: Theresa Martin

TREE HOUSE DINING ROOM

Tree House Dining Room Mat board was cut in detail to create the roots at the bottom of the Tree House, which reach down into the dining room.

Hotel Lobby The back wall of the Hotel lobby is created with one piece of mat board, into which archways are cut. The mat board replaces the entire back piece of wood from the cigar box. Once the mat board was glued into place, the entire box and mat board was painted to unify the look. The archways look out to a photo of the Taj Mahal, which was backed with cardstock for stability and then adhered to the box exterior with linen tape to keep it in place. The photo is curved outward to provide a three-dimensional effect.

Gothic House Living Room The arches framing the hallway of the Gothic House living room were created from mat board. The arches were drawn onto the mat board, cut out with a craft knife, and painted and embellished, before being adhered to the box.

GOTHIC HOUSE LIVING ROOM

HOTEL LOBBY

The No Cutting, Faux Cutting Method

IF YOU'RE REALLY NOT A FAN of cutting, you can still create the illusion of windows, doors, and other features without all the hard work.

◆ Create faux windows by cutting out the inner, "window" portion of a rubber-stamped or printed window-frame image. Place an image behind the frame to create your own view. Use foam adhesive tape between your window image and the "view" behind it to add a three-dimensional effect.

◆ Use miniature wooden windows, available from dollhouse shops and craft stores.

◆ Draw your own windows from paper and cut them out or use our template in the Appendix on page 122. You can also use stamped or clip art images.

◆ Frame a faux window with paper shutters cut from cardstock, with leftover wood cutouts (or use our template in the Appendix on page 124). Add a fold or small hinge to allow them to open and close.

◆ Create a working door by cutting a door from cardstock and adding a 1" (2.5 cm) tab to one side. Fold along the line that marks the edge of the door and the tab. The fold line will act as the "hinge" for your door. Adhere the tab to the wall of the assemblage.

◆ Instead of a complicated door or window, consider creating an open archway.

◆ To fill your window and door frames, adhere images of landscapes, cityscapes, or other scenes that you would see from a window or door behind the frames. You can also use your own photographs or painted images. Check out window and door catalogs from local hardware stores or installers for realistic images, or go through your junk mail. Cut out images to use in your assemblage.

THE HOTEL PENTHOUSE WINDOWS

Artist: Theresa Martin

Faking It

Artist: Tally Oliveau

EXTERIOR WINDOWS OF THE HOTEL'S HONEYMOON SUITE

Hotel Penthouse A window was created in the Hotel penthouse by adhering two city-view photos to the back wall. Handmade window treatments were attached to either side of the photos, covering the edges.

Heartbreak Hotel Room In the Hotel's Heartbreak Hotel Room, a dollhouse window frame with panes was painted and adhered over an emotional image that conveys a particular message to the viewer. Fabric curtains were hung on either side of the window frame.

HEARTBREAK HOTEL ROOM WINDOW

Artist: Paula Dion

Tip Paint, paper, and embellish your doors, windows, shutters, and other inserts before adhering them to your assemblage.

Faking It

CIRCUS HOUSE SIDESHOW ROOM WINDOW

Hotel Honeymoon Suite (page 33)

Because you don't have an actual cutout when you're faking it, the inside and outside of your assemblage don't necessarily have to match. The Honeymoon Suite, for example, has faux windows on the outside of the assemblage but no corresponding windows on the inside of the room—which is perfectly okay. Of course, if you have a cutout in the box, the cutout will need to be incorporated into both sides of your piece.

Circus House Sideshow Room A

window frame cut from black paper was adhered to the wall in the Circus House Sideshow Room. Images conveying the artist's message were placed behind and around the frame. A door was added in this manner, as well.

Circus House Nightmare Room A

door image was simply adhered to the side wall in the Circus House Nightmare Room—no power tools, no craft knives.

The Hotel Lost and Found A painted,

miniature wooden window frame with panes was adhered over a photo of an eye looking into the Hotel Lost and Found.

CIRCUS HOUSE NIGHTMARE ROOM DOOR

THE HOTEL LOST AND FOUND WINDOW

Creating Moldings and Window Frames

To create moldings and edges for your window frames, cut paper, cardstock, or even mat board into long, thin rectangles and glue them to the "walls" with tacky glue or gel medium. To add dimension to the framing, use adhesive foam tape to adhere the pieces. If you have rubber stamps of window-frame images, these can also be used. Stamp the images onto cardstock or mat board, cut them out, and adhere them. Another option is to buy miniature wood molding from a dollhouse supply store or craft store. These can be easily cut to size with scissors or wire cutters. Or, just use one of our templates in the Appendix, on page 122.

3 The First Layers

Once the basic structure of your assemblage is complete, you are ready to apply the first layers of actual art. There are so many options for covering your plain wooden box that the process can actually be overwhelming. But before you dive in, keep in mind that there's no reason you can't leave all, or even a portion, of your assemblage box bare, and, if you're using cigar boxes already covered with cool-looking papers, you might want to keep them as they are.

If you do want more than a bare assemblage box, you can narrow down your options for covering it to paint and paper. Painting the box retains the wood texture, which can be an important part of the feel of your assemblage. Depending on your abilities or confidence with a paintbrush, the sky's the limit for the looks you can achieve. Covering the box with paper provides a smooth, even finish; alternatively, using torn paper or tissue paper can give the box surface texture. Unlike painting, which can require some planning and labor to achieve the look you want, using paper to cover your box is quick and provides immediate gratification. With the myriad papers available at craft and scrapbooking stores, finding just the right paper to suit the theme and style of your assemblage is not likely to be difficult.

exterior
layered with paper
and molding paste

layer
with paint

layer
with collage

Artist: Deryn Mentock

Using Paint

YOU DON'T REALLY NEED TO PRIME wooden boxes before you paint them, but a coat of gesso can help even out surfaces and color tones. You also don't need to use expensive paints. Inexpensive acrylic paints do a good job of covering most wood, cardboard, and paper surfaces. They're easy to use, come in a wide variety of colors, clean up easily with soap and water, are mostly nontoxic, and dry quickly. If you want your acrylic paint to dry more slowly, to allow you to blend colors, mix an extender, such as gel medium, into the paint.

Layering Paint Colors

The colors you choose for the inside and outside of your assemblage will have a significant effect on the look and feel of your piece. In our dollhouse project, for example, blues and greens were used for the insides and outsides of the Under the Sea House boxes. Similarly, the outside of the Gothic House was painted black. Choose colors that match the theme, concept, or feeling that you want to convey in your assemblage.

Once you've decided on a basic color scheme, brush your chosen color or colors over the surface of your box. To create layered color, begin by painting the exterior a single color. Once your first layer of paint is dry, dip a relatively dry brush into a complementary paint color and brush it over the first color, letting some of the first layer of paint show through. Using this dry-brushing technique to paint on two or three additional layers of color can create a more interesting and dimensional background. Be sure to let each layer of paint dry before adding the next—you want to layer the colors, not mix them into a muddy mess.

POSSIBILITIES FOR PAPER AND PAINT TO DECORATE YOUR DOLLHOUSE ROOMS ARE ALMOST LIMITLESS.

Tip To achieve a uniform assemblage exterior for a large enclosure or multiple enclosures, paint all exteriors at the same time, especially if you are mixing custom paint colors. You might even want to temporarily connect the enclosures in their final assemblage configuration before you paint, so that your brush strokes evenly and naturally pass over the separate pieces, unifying them. The backgrounds and exteriors of your assemblage set the tone for the rest of your artwork and are integral to your piece. Take the time to plan, prepare, and implement your first layers.

Using Paint

BLACK EXTERIORS OF THE GOTHIC HOUSE

PAINTED EXTERIOR OF THE UNDER THE SEA HOUSE TREASURE ROOM

Artist: Tally Oliveau

CASTLE AVIARY EXTERIOR

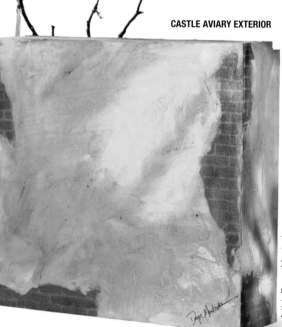

Artist: Deryn Mentock

Gothic House Most of the Gothic House exteriors are painted a simple black, to fit the gothic theme. Simple can be good; you can always add paint and other textures or features later.

Under the Sea House Treasure Room The exterior of this room combines shades of blue and green. The layers of complementary colors, brushed on in long, horizontal strokes, are reminiscent of the ocean. Some of the rooms in this house are covered with layers of paper in blue hues, which evoke water and its movement.

Castle Aviary Exterior Pieces of brick-patterned paper were intermixed with molding paste to create the exterior of the Castle aviary. Acrylic paint was used on the molding paste, and glaze was applied over the exterior, to give it a uniform look. The final effect is of an aged-brick wall.

Castle Library "Stones," befitting the Castle theme, were painted onto the exterior of the Castle library. The look was achieved by first painting the box gray and then lightly sponging white and black acrylic paints over the gray. The outlines of the stones were drawn with a black Sharpie pen in a random pattern, to look like real stones; the "grout" between the stones was filled in with the same black Sharpie.

Castle Attic For the Castle attic exterior, pages from the book *Rapunzel* were torn into stone shapes and collaged onto the assemblage exterior. Glaze was painted over the collaged paper and allowed to seep into the crevices and torn paper edges, to enhance the spaces between the "stones." The paint glaze unifies the papers and transforms them from torn pieces of paper to stones in the rotunda wall.

The Castle Because our dollhouse project was collaborative, the stone exteriors of the Castle were created by different artists and are therefore not all the same. The paint colors are also not a match. But this is the look we were going for. In fact, real castles were often built over a long period of time, with consecutive owners adding onto the original structure using different architectural styles and materials.

PAPER AND PAINTED GLAZE "STONES" OF THE CASTLE ATTIC AND LIBRARY EXTERIORS

THE ECLECTIC EXTERIOR OF THE CASTLE
(CLOSE UP)

Using Paper

ANOTHER OPTION FOR COVERING your assemblage box, whether it's the inside or the outside, is using decorative paper. Papering the outside of your assemblage covers the plain wood and gives the box a finished look. Papering the inside of the assemblage provides wallpaper for a room and a background surface for texture and design, similar to its use in collage.

Craft and scrapbooking stores are crammed with a huge selection of decorative papers and cardstocks that can provide instant color, pattern, and design. Other papers you can use to create unique and unusual designs include wrapping paper, tissue paper, wallpaper samples, paper torn from old books or ledgers, music sheets, magazines and catalogs, and collaged or stamped papers that you've designed and created yourself.

When planning your assemblage, choose papers that fit your theme. For example, if you're creating a Bohemian gypsy room, choose papers with funky, Bohemian designs, bright colors, and swirly florals. A jungle safari room calls for papers in greens, browns, and animal prints. But you can also use papers in plant prints, magazine photos of grass and leaves, or, even better, your own photographs or drawings.

Papers, like paint, also help your assemblage convey a particular mood; choose papers in colors that complement that mood. Bright colors and prints, for example, evoke a different mood than dark, somber colors.

Getting Smooth Coverage

To achieve a smooth surface when applying paper to the box, squeeze a dollop of adhesive, such as soft gel medium or a strong tacky glue, onto the paper. Use a paintbrush or the edge of an old credit card to spread the glue thinly and evenly over the surface—this helps prevent your paper from buckling. Lay the paper carefully onto the box and immediately roll a brayer over it to smooth it out.

Getting clean edges can be tricky. You want the edges of the paper covering the assemblage walls to match up cleanly to each other and to the edges of the box. One option is to measure and cut all your paper pieces at once with a paper cutter, which always leaves a nice, clean edge, rather than gluing the pieces on and then trying to cut them with a craft knife. You can also cut the paper slightly larger than the area to be covered and fold the extra paper over, or around, the inside corners or outside edges of the box. A third option is to cover the entire inside or outside of the box with one large, continuous piece of paper. The paper can cover all the inside corners or outside edges of the assemblage, providing an even, uninterrupted surface.

Creating Smooth Corners and Edges

1 **Cut a piece of paper** slightly wider than the width of the side wall and adhere it to the box with gel medium. Fold the excess paper over the inside edge of the box, to create a tab, and adhere it. When using this technique for the outside of a box, fold the excess paper tab over and around the box's edge.

2 **Adhere another piece of paper over the tab** to create a clean corner or edge.

FOR THE TREE HOUSE LIVING ROOM, TWO PIECES OF PAPER WERE MERGED TO CREATE A CLEAN EDGE.

Artist: Debrina Pratt

THE PRINTED PAPER MAKING UP THE BACKGROUND OF THE CASTLE LIBRARY IS ONE CONTINUOUS PIECE OF PAPER.

Artist: Tally Oliveau

Mitering Corners

Mitering is a simple, effective way to create clean corners over any surface. For this example, a piece of wood from a cigar box is used. This technique can be used to cover mat board, a book cover, or any other flat surface.

2 **Fold the top edge of the paper** onto your piece and glue it down, then fold over the side edge and adhere it.

1 **Cut a piece of paper** 1–1½" (2.5–3.8 cm) longer and wider than the surface to be covered. The excess paper will be folded over your piece of wood or mat board. Place the wood or board piece on the "wrong" side of the paper, being sure to leave excess paper on each side. With scissors, cut off one corner of the paper, approximately ⅛" (3 mm) from the edge of the piece.

3 **Your mitered corner** is complete!

Creating Three-Dimensional Interest

Paper, foam tape, molding paste, and even bathroom caulking can be used to add dimension to your assemblage. Papers can be used to create dimension by layering them with foam tape. The tape not only supports the papers, it also lifts them off the background papers. To add even more interest, expose your layers by offsetting them.

Use molding paste or bathroom caulking by spreading a thick layer onto your surface and using texturizing tools or even your fingers, to create texture or designs in the paste. To create a transition and hide hard lines between papers or paper and paint, use a plastic or palette knife to slather molding paste or caulking over the edges of the paper on the box. Spread and smoosh it with your fingers, texturing tool, or comb.

Paper Collage

Once you have painted or papered the exterior of your assemblage box, it's time to turn to the interiors. To add interest and give the piece depth of meaning, create a collage to place within your assemblage. The collage provides another way to tell your story and convey your message. Your collage can be a complex collection of papers, paints, and rubber stamping or a simple combination of coordinating patterned papers that fit your theme.

Paper
Background Layers

GOTHIC HOUSE LIVING ROOM

Artist: Debrina Pratt

CASTLE DUNGEON

Artist: Lisa Myers-Bulmash

Gothic House Living Room The imposing figures of the statues are flat images printed on white paper and inked at the edges to create depth. The affect is dramatic against the baroque grey-and-red patterned wallpaper.

Castle Dungeon The brick-patterned paper in the Castle dungeon gives the space its raw ambiance.

Wonderland House Attic Creative use of space images cut from science magazines give the Wonderland House attic a mysterious feel. The space images convey the idea that the possibilities of the mind are as limitless as the possibilities in outer space.

Artist: Tally Oliveau

WONDERLAND HOUSE ATTIC

Paper
Three-Dimensional Interest

Artist: Theresa Martin

UNDER THE SEA HOUSE DINING ROOM

Under the Sea House Dining Room

Paper was used to create some of the furniture and architectural trimmings for the Under the Sea House dining room. Grecian columns (with cool fish heads!) were printed onto cardstock, cut out, and adhered with dimensional foam tape. Sturdy decorative paper was cut and folded for the dining table and window frames, which stand away from the images in the windows. This effect was achieved by attaching the window frames with foam tape.

Hotel Lollipop Shop
The Hotel Lollipop Shop's paper circle cutouts were adhered to the back of the assemblage with dimensional foam tape.

Wonderland House Nursery
For the nursery in the Wonderland House, the artist used real candy wrappers and paper cupcake cups, befitting the theme.

Artist: Debrina Pratt

HOTEL LOLLIPOP SHOP

Artist: Caryl Hoobler

WONDERLAND HOUSE NURSERY

Paper
Paper Collage

Artist: Julie Molina

**WONDERLAND HOUSE
MUSIC BOX ROOM COLLAGE**

Wonderland House Music Box Room

Rather than use a single sheet of paper to cover the background of the Wonderland House Music Box Room, the artist used several different patterned papers, some with musical notes, to suit the theme. Swirls were drawn, cut out and then adhered to the assemblage in both flat and three-dimensional ways, adding to the background effect.

Hotel Honeymoon Suite
A small collage was added to the background in the Hotel's Honeymoon Suite. The collage was assembled on a piece of cardstock measured and cut to fit inside the assemblage. Images of houses, hearts, babies, and other dreams and thoughts that might transpire between two newlyweds early in their married life were included in the collage, which was adhered to the assemblage with foam tape.

Wonderland Dining Room
The rear wall of the Wonderland dining room uses collage to great effect and offers some humor, to boot! Images of an open mouth, a woman serving food, and boxes of Spam are put together in a clever, tongue-in-cheek manner.

Castle Aviary
All of the Castle aviary interior walls are collaged with patterned papers, rubber-stamped images, and handwritten notes from the artist. Vintage images of caged birds run across the top of the background, relating to the assemblage theme.

THE WONDERLAND DINING ROOM COLLAGE ADDS HUMOR.

HOTEL HONEYMOON SUITE COLLAGE

**BIRDS REIGN IN
THE CASTLE AVIARY
INTERIORS.**

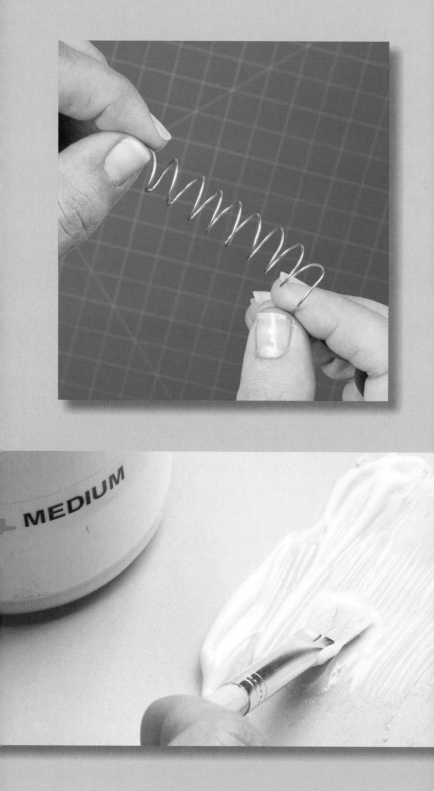

4 Getting Attached

When you adhere something in your assemblage, you want it to stay there—forever. Paper dolls should not fall over, metal pieces should not pull off, and paper should not buckle or peel. One of the most important aspects of creating your assemblage is making sure that everything stays where you want it.

The two methods of "getting attached" covered in this book are using adhesives and cold joining. Adhesives include glues, gel mediums, and tape. Cold joining, a term used in the jewelry trade that we're borrowing for assemblage, joins materials or items without soldering, using instead materials such as wire, bolts, and nails.

Soldering is another widely used technique for permanently joining two or more objects, and it's used extensively in making jewelry. Soldering requires high heat, special tools, and a lot of practice. Although soldering is not covered in this book, if you are already comfortable with it, you can use this technique for your assemblage projects.

paper glaze
adhesive

double
sided foam tape

gel
medium

TREASURE IN THE UNDER THE SEA HOUSE TREASURE ROOM

Artist: Tally Oliveau

Using Adhesives

PROBABLY THE FASTEST, easiest, and least expensive way to join papers and lightweight materials is to use adhesives. There are many different types of adhesives—from simple glue sticks, for gluing paper to paper, to heavy-duty glues, for adhering heavier objects, such as charms and other three-dimensional pieces—and choosing the right one for the job can be confusing. We've provided a brief primer on some of our favorites here.

ADHESIVES COME IN MANY FORMS, FROM GLUE STICKS TO GEL MEDIUM AND FOAM TAPE. USE WHAT WORKS BEST FOR YOUR PROJECT.

Glue Sticks

Glue sticks are an inexpensive and easy-to-use adhesive for paper, and many are acid-free. Because glue sticks are not as "wet" as gel medium and tacky glue when applied, they are a good choice for adhering delicate lace or tissue papers, and there's no wait for it to dry. However, glue sticks are not as permanent as the other adhesive options described in this section.

Gel Medium

Gel medium is commonly used by many artists. Slightly thicker than basic white glue, gel medium is acid-free and permanent and can be used in many applications in addition to being an adhesive: as a medium for creating texture, as an extender for acrylic paints, and for sealing paper projects and finished acrylic or collage pieces. Soft gel medium can even be used for image transfers.

Gel medium is available in a variety of thicknesses—soft gel, medium body, and heavy body—and can be used for different applications. Do you want to create a deep texture? Use heavy body gel medium. Are you looking for a smooth, seamless surface under paper? Use soft gel medium. You can also choose from three finishes: matte, gloss, and semi-gloss.

Gel medium works well for paper, metal, and wood and can be used in your assemblage project to glue boxes together or to glue mat board pieces into your assemblage. Use a cheap paintbrush to apply the medium, and, when you're done, clean the brush with plain water.

Tacky Glue

Tacky glue is a great alternative to basic white glue and even gel medium. Tacky glue is stronger than white glue, but is thinner and not as strong as gel medium. Because it's a thinner glue, it also dries faster than gel medium. Use tacky glue for adhering paper and small, lightweight, detail items that need to dry quickly. Perfect Paper Adhesive (PPA) is an example of a tacky glue that works well for paper. PPA is archival and acid-free and dries transparent. It is also available in matte and glossy finishes and, like gel medium, can be used as a sealer. Use it straight from the bottle or apply it with a cheap paintbrush.

Dimensional Adhesive

Dimensional adhesive dries to a clear, hard, plastic consistency and adds dimension to flat surfaces or items. Squeeze a small, three-dimensional "drop" onto any flat surface, and it will dry that way—as a hard, plastic bubble. Use this adhesive to fill in bezels or to cover and seal images or words. Be sure to avoid disturbing the adhesive during the required drying time, so you don't ruin your perfect bubble. Although this adhesive looks milky when it's wet, it dries clear and nearly invisible, with a glossy finish.

Dimensional adhesive is also a strong, permanent glue for use with paper, metal, wood, mica, and even glass. It can be expensive, however, so you might want to use it for smaller areas. Several types of dimensional adhesives are available, including Inkssentials Glossy Accents, JudiKins Diamond Glaze, and Aleene's Paper Glaze.

Gorilla Glue

Gorilla Glue is a super-strong, permanent glue that works well on metal and wood and for adhering large or heavy items that you want to be sure will *never* move. Be careful when using Gorilla Glue: as it dries, it can bubble out from underneath your object. Be sure to wipe away these bubbles as they form—unless you really want rock-solid, brown glue bubbles surrounding your object. Use a baby wipe or wet towel for clean wiping.

E-6000

E-6000 is an industrial-strength, permanent glue commonly used in jewelry making. It dries clear and is ideal for use with metal, plastic, and other slick surfaces. Use this adhesive only when others won't work, following the manufacturer's recommendations carefully. It should always be used in a well-ventilated area (preferably outside) and with latex or other protective gloves to prevent skin contact. When using E-6000, allow your art piece to dry for 24 to 48 hours in a well-ventilated room.

Tip When in doubt, test a new glue before using it in an art piece for the first time.

Glue Dots

Glue dots are very sticky "buttons" of glue that provide a strong hold for oddly shaped items. Available on a roll or sheet, glue dots are sticky on both sides and come in various glue strengths and sizes, which means that, unlike double-sided tape, they don't need to be cut to size. Glue dots provide an instant bond and are an excellent choice for adhering ribbons, beads, small objects (such as buttons and charms), and highly textured papers into your assemblage.

Double-Sided Tape

If you're concerned about having thin papers buckle when using a wet glue, try double-sided tape, such as Scotch brand double-sided tape. This tape holds well and doesn't show through most papers (though it will show through transparent papers, such as vellum). For adhering materials and objects that require a stronger hold, a tackier double-sided tape, such as Red Line Tape, is recommended. It's available in varying widths and can even be embossed.

Dimensional Foam Tape

Dimensional foam tape is a thick, double-sided tape that is used to add dimension—it "pops up" the object or paper you're adhering. Dimensional foam tape provides a strong hold, doesn't make papers buckle, and gives a three-dimensional effect to layered papers. You can stack multiple layers of the tape to get the height you're looking for. Foam tape is available in strips and in "dots" or small squares, for smaller items.

Linen Tape

Linen tape can usually be found in the bookmaking section of arts and craft stores. Use this acid-free tape for joining sections of your assemblage frame without the need for wet glue. Linen tape creates a strong hold and provides a smooth transition when used to connect different materials, such as cigar box pieces and mat board pieces.

Other Tapes

Tape has come a long way since the days of plain, old beige masking tape. Many home-renovation and art-supply stores now carry masking tape in many colors; tapes printed with graphic designs and even words are also available. Other tapes to consider using are metallic tapes, stained-glass-window tapes (usually available in silver, brass and copper), and even duct tape! Use tape as a background, for example, instead of paint or paper, or use it as a border-design element. Unusual tapes can add great interest and texture to your assemblage.

IMMEDIATELY LAY THE PAPER ONTO YOUR BOX (OR OTHER SURFACE) AND USE YOUR BRAYER TO SMOOTH IT DOWN TO ENSURE GOOD ADHESION.

Using Cold Joins

COLD JOINING IS A METHOD OF JOINING materials or items without using glue, tape, or solder. Although glue is the easiest way to adhere materials together, it isn't always the best way. If your object is too delicate, doesn't have enough surface area for glue or tape, needs to be moveable, or is too slick for a glue to grip, your best option is to use cold joining. Objects can be attached to your assemblage with wire, bolts, or nails.

Wire

A simple and common cold-joining technique is wire wrapping. An object is wrapped with wire then wired to the assemblage wall. For the Tree House attic, for example, plastic tree forms were attached to the side of the assemblage box by passing craft wire through a hole drilled into the side of the box and then wire wrapping the plastic tree form to the box.

Wire can also be used to attach objects to an assemblage by simply encircling the two objects to be joined and twisting the wire on itself to close it. (It's like using a twist tie to close up a bread bag.) You can also use wire to make your own jump rings, which can be used to attach objects into your assemblage.

The best gauges to use for cold joining are from 22 to 18 (the smaller the gauge number, the thicker the wire). At these gauges, the wire will be easy to wrap but still strong enough to hold your pieces in place. Along with the wire's gauge, consider the wire color. Wires come in a rainbow of colors, now, allowing you to coordinate your wire with the colors and theme of your art piece. Gold tones might call for brass- or copper-colored wire. A silver wire might coordinate nicely with turquoise or green. Decide whether you want your wire to be camouflaged or whether you want it to stand out, as another design element.

Securing Items with Wire Wrapping

1 **Determine where you want to make your attachment** and drill a hole into your assemblage. Pass your craft wire through the hole.

2 **Wrap the wire around the object** you want to attach, passing the craft wire through your drilled hole each time you wrap it around your object.

3 **Neatly cut the end of your craft wire** and tuck it under one of your wrap layers to conceal it and prevent it from snagging. This gives a professional and clean finished look.

Wire Springs

Handmade wire springs can be used to attach objects to your assemblage in a whimsical way. Wire springs are perfect for attaching butterflies, birds, jack-in-the-box heads, and any other objects that need slight movement or just the impression of movement. These springs are easy to make. Use a craft wire with a gauge between 22 and 18.

To wire wrap an object that's not near the edge of your assemblage, you'll need to drill two holes through the box, spaced apart slightly less than the width of the object to be attached, so that the object at least partially masks the holes. Once the holes are drilled, place the object between the two holes; pass the wire through one hole, over the object, and through the second hole. Then pass the wire back through the first hole, around and again through the second hole. Holding the two ends of your wire together between wraps, pull the wire toward you to tighten the wrap then continue wrapping, repeating the steps above. Keep wrapping your wire around and over the object then through your two holes until you feel satisfied that your object is attached firmly.

Making Wire Springs

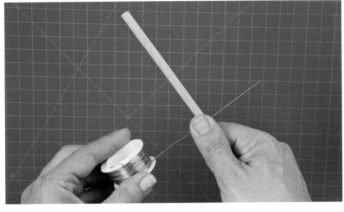

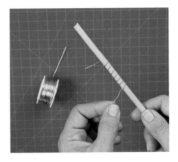

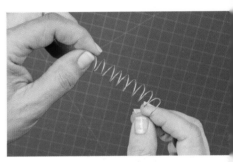

1 **Using your finger,** hold one end of your wire against a dowel, pencil, or other cylindrical object of desired diameter. Leave a small straight piece, about ½" (1.3 cm) long, at the start of the wire, before you begin wrapping, to serve as a point of attachment.

2 **Wrap the wire tightly around the dowel** until you are happy with the length of the spring. If you discover later that the spring is too long, you can easily cut off the excess.

3 **Carefully pull the wrapped wire off the dowel,** to reveal the spring. Cut the spring from the remaining wire, leaving another tail at this end. One tail will attach to your object; the other will be attached to your assemblage.

Nails and Bolts

Items can also be nailed or bolted directly into your assemblage structure. Use nails when the items you want to attach can be directly nailed into your assemblage (such as wood) or that are heavy or difficult to glue or tape into your assemblage. Finishing nails, used in carpentry, are a good choice for nailing items, because they are small and can be nailed all the way into an object. The nail head can then be covered with spackle and painted, so that it doesn't show.

To wire wrap an object to a nail, use a nail with a head, and be sure that enough of the nail head is exposed to allow space for the wrap. If a nail is too long or extends past the outside of your box, cut the end off with metal shears or a wire cutter.

Bolts are bulkier than nails but can add a great industrial look to your assemblage. When drilling the hole for the bolt, be sure to use a drill bit with a large enough diameter to allow the bolt to slip through the hole. Once the bolt is fitted into the assemblage, secure it with a corresponding nut.

Tip Pulling apart the ends of the spring lengthens it and creates a looser spring. To maintain a tight spring, wrap the wire closely around the dowel and try not to pull the ends away from each other when removing the spring from the dowel.

Attachments
Adhesives

Artist: Gale Blair

THE TREE HOUSE ATTIC

Artist: Theresa Martin

THE CIRCUS HOUSE ATTIC

Tree House Attic The paper dolls in the Tree House attic were attached with foam tape to make them stand away from the back wall and provide a three-dimensional effect.

Circus House Attic Glue was used to join the wood pieces making up the attic outer walls and rooftop and to adhere the jack-in-the-box bases to the floor.

WIRE-WRAPPED COLD JOIN ONTO NAILS IN LOST AND FOUND ROOM

Cold Joins

Hotel Lost and Found
The antique porcelain doll in the Hotel Lost and Found was wire wrapped into the assemblage. Copper craft wire was wound around the arms and legs of the porcelain doll and then wound around nails hammered into the sides and floor of the assemblage. The wire wrapping around the doll was used not just as an attachment in this piece but also as part of its message and artistry (see page 78). The figure is tied down, both figuratively and physically. Although it appears to be running away, it cannot release itself from its ties. Only the insect wings manage to release themselves and fly away. Whether they become lost or found is up to the viewer.

Castle Dungeon
For the Castle dungeon, the heavy, "tortured figure" piece (made from an altered medicine bottle) was bolted into the assemblage. Corresponding holes were drilled through the medicine bottle and the bottom of the box with a rotary tool, and a bolt was inserted through the holes to secure the piece.

Nightmare Clown Room
To make the scary nightmare clowns move, they were attached to the back of the assemblage wall with springs. Dimensional adhesive was used to attach the springs to the back wall, and foam tape was used to attach the other end of the spring to each clown head, providing additional stability to the paper.

THE CASTLE DUNGEON TORTURED FIGURE

NIGHTMARE CLOWN ROOM CLOWNS

(Continued, page 60)

(Continued from page 59)

Tree House Attic The stars in the Tree House attic shoot through the sky on aged springs. The springs were attached to the ceiling of the assemblage by gluing the tail end of the spring into a small hole, which was partially drilled through the top of the box. The other end of the spring was attached to the star with gel medium.

Circus House Attic The Circus House attic jack-in-the-boxes would simply be incomplete without their heads on springs! One end of each spring was glued into a hole partially drilled into each wooden base; the other end was attached to the clown head with gel medium.

Castle Bedroom The bird is tethered to the princess's hand with a coiled wire. The bird is adhered to the wire with glue dots and tape. The other end of the wire was wrapped around the princess's hand.

The Tree House Pondering Room
The bamboo cage chair is able to swing because it is wired into a hole through the ceiling. Extra beads were strung on the wire to the left of the swing for decorative effect.

Artist: Gale Blair

TREE HOUSE ATTIC STARS

CIRCUS HOUSE ATTIC JACK-IN-THE BOX CLOWNS

Artist: Theresa Martin

CASTLE BEDROOM BIRD

Artist: Debrina Pratt

Artist: Julie Molina

PONDERING ROOM

Cool Dangly Things

HAVING MOVEMENT IN YOUR ASSEMBLAGE provides a surprise for the viewer and adds interest to your artwork. The movement can be subtle, such as a piece that dangles from the ceiling. You can also include movement that provides an opportunity for the viewer to interact with pieces in your assemblage. Many of the rooms in our dollhouse project include pieces that move, such as dangly chandeliers and swinging trapeze artists. Other items that naturally lend themselves to movement and dangling include those that naturally "hang" in the sky, such as stars, clouds, the sun, or the moon; objects that fly, such as birds, butterflies, and other winged creatures; and objects that hang, such as swings and wind chimes.

Artist: Julie Molina

A FABRIC DOLL SOARS IN THE CIRCUS HOUSE TRAPEZE ROOM.

Attaching Danglies

To camouflage the line and make your dangly appear to float or move on its own, use fishing line or clear, thin thread. Objects can also be suspended from eye pins commonly used in jewelry making. Attached to the top or side of your assemblage, an eye pin can serve as a place to attach a dangly using a jump ring.

To attach a dangly to your assemblage, you'll first need to pass the eye pin through a small hole in the box. Drill the hole using a rotary tool with a very fine drill bit, or, if you're using a cigar box, you can make the hole with an awl, gently and slowly pushed through the soft wood. Pass the pin through the hole, making sure the eye is on the side of the box where you want to make your attachment. Snugging the eye up against the box, bend the shaft of the pin flat against the other side of the box and adhere it with tape. Conceal the bent pin shaft by covering it with decorative paper.

You can dangle an object inside and outside of your assemblage from the same attachment by using a double-ended eye pin made from wire. Cut a 3"–5" (7.6–12.7 cm) piece of 22–18 gauge wire and, using round-nose pliers, make a loop at one end of the wire. Pass the other end of the wire through the hole in the assemblage wall. Pull the first loop snug against the side of the box then cut off the excess wire, leaving only enough wire to make another loop. Make a loop from the remaining wire and snug it against the other side of the assemblage wall, anchoring it. You can attach your dangly piece to either side of your assemblage using a jump ring.

CRYSTAL BALLS IN THE UNDER THE SEA BEDROOM

Under the Sea Bedroom

Crystal balls—really beads—hang from the ceiling in the Under the Sea bedroom. Wire was passed through each bead until the bead rested midway along the length of the wire. The wire was then folded into a U-shape and passed through a small hole drilled through the top of the cigar box to the exterior, where it was twisted to keep it to the desired length. The twisted wire was then folded flat against the surface of the box, adhered with tape, and covered with decorative paper.

Circus House Trapeze Room

A hand-sewn fabric doll and plastic ballerinas dangle in the Circus House Trapeze Room. They are all attached with wire and tacky glue.

(Continued, page 64)

Artist: Lisa Myers-Bulmash

DANGLING LEAF BEADS IN THE TREE HOUSE BEDROOM

**KNOTS IN FISHING LINE ON THE OUTSIDE OF THE TREE HOUSE BEDROOM
HOLD THE DANGLING LEAVES IN PLACE (VIEW FROM TOP).**

Tree House Bedroom To create the dangling leaves in the Tree House bedroom, one end of a piece of fishing line was tied to each bead. The other end was passed through a small hole in the top of the box.

On the outside of the box, the fishing line was knotted several times, to hold it in place and to ensure that the knot was thick enough to keep the fishing line from slipping back through the hole.

A TRAPEZE ARTIST AT WORK IN THE CIRCUS HOUSE SIDESHOW ROOM

Circus House Sideshow Room

Jewelry thread with a rope-like texture was used to dangle the trapeze artist in the Circus House Sideshow room. One end of the thread was wrapped and tied around a small nail hammered into the ceiling of the assemblage and then sealed with dimensional adhesive. The other end of the thread was attached to the assemblage ceiling with glue. The paper curtain at the front of the assemblage cleverly conceals and seals the end of the thread.

Castle Dining Room, Bedroom, and Living Room

The chandeliers in these rooms were made from jewelry findings and beads, attached with eye pins. The chandeliers were attached to the eye pins with jump rings.

A GLITTERING CHANDELIER IN THE CASTLE BEDROOM

5 Paper Dolls and Beyond

Including paper dolls and other figures

in your assemblage can help round out your theme and make your ideas come to life. A fantasy living space isn't complete without characters to help you tell your story. Why not put some ghosts in the attic, princesses in the castle, and even birds and monkeys in that tree house? After all, who says your dolls have to be people? They might be animals or half-human and half-bird. They might even be fish.

Finding Inspiration

WHEN LOOKING FOR INSPIRATION, a good place to start is with vintage photos, collage sheets, and paper-doll books. There are many resources for images: some are available on CD; others can be downloaded from online sites and printed out. Check out pages 120–121 in the Appendix, for a few copyright-free cabinet cards from our own collections for your personal use. Plus, more—you'll also find paper doll templates!

Clip-art books are another source, as are books of royalty-free images from publishers such as Dover. If you have cabinet cards stashed away in a drawer, this is a good time to use them. You can also use family photos—both vintage and current—photos from magazines and catalogs, images of classical paintings, rubber-stamped images, and even your own drawings.

When looking for an image to use as the base for your paper doll, be sure that your character has, at the least, a complete head and neck. Complete shoulders are a bonus but are easier to draw in, if they're missing, than a neck. Your character does not need to have a body; drawing your own body helps to personalize your paper doll.

You might have to scan and resize your paper-doll images, using your computer. But you don't necessarily need to be confined by the walls of your assemblage. Your doll might be like Alice and has grown too large for your room. Maybe her hands and feet are sticking out of the windows.

VINTAGE COLLAGE SHEETS (MAINLY FOUND ONLINE), CLIP-ART BOOKS, AND CABINET CARDS OFFER LOTS OF INSPIRATION FOR CREATING PAPER DOLLS.

Tip Unsure of your drawing skills? Find a complete, full-body image and use the whole image for your paper doll.

Making a Doll

This paper doll is made using a vintage cabinet-card image, which was scanned into a computer and printed onto acid-free paper. Using the head and body outline from your original image, you can create a paper doll with new paper clothes that fit perfectly.

Materials

- ◆ image to use as the base for your paper doll
- ◆ pencil
- ◆ paper
- ◆ decorative paper
- ◆ tracing paper
- ◆ scissors
- ◆ embellishments

1 **To ensure that your new paper clothes fit your paper doll,** begin by drawing a pencil outline of your original image's figure onto tracing paper. If you are creating new hair, you will also need to trace around the shape of the head. If you are just creating new clothes, begin drawing at the neckline, where your new collar and shoulders will begin. You do not need to trace the body parts you are going to leave as is, such as the face and arms. For this example, only the clothes of the original cabinet-card image will be altered, so the face and neck are left as is. Once the shoulders and neckline have been traced, the rest of the dress will be drawn freehand.

2 **Cut around your printed copy** of the head and neck image, leaving what you'd like to keep and cutting into the hair or body to make room for a new hairdo, hat, wings or whatever creative changes and embellishments you want to add. Be sure to leave a large base of paper below the head, neck, and shoulders of your paper doll, so that you can easily attach the new body or clothes.

3 **Place the tracing paper** with your pencil drawing of the doll's body, pencil side down, onto the *reverse* side

of your patterned paper (the paper you're using for the doll's clothes) and retrace your pencil marks. This will transfer your pencil marks from the tracing paper to the reverse side of the patterned paper.

4 **Cut out the shape of the dress** (or other clothing) to the correct size of your paper doll. When you turn the patterned paper back to the correct side, you will have no pencil marks, and the shape will be to size.

Use this same technique to change your paper doll's hair. With the tracing paper over your face image, trace the head shape and draw on an outline of your new hair design. Flip the tracing paper over, pencil side down onto the *reverse* side of the paper you want to use for the hair, and retrace your lines to transfer the pencil

marks onto the paper. Then cut out the new hair shape, which should fit perfectly onto your paper doll's head.

5 **Finish your doll with embellishments,** such as a brass crown, tin roses, and German scrap.

 Tip By scanning your image, you can use it many times, in different sizes, without destroying your original.

Tip The computer is an excellent tool for manipulating and making adjustments to your images, such as changing the size, making copies, or creating effects with image-processing software, such as Adobe Photoshop. The software can also help you create your dolls with less work. For example, you can scan an image into your computer and do the cutting and pasting electronically. The software can also help you create dolls from your own drawings. If the thought of using image-processing software worries you, don't fret—you can still make these dolls the old-fashioned way, with good old scissors, paper, and adhesive.

Standing Tall

Once you've created your doll, you'll want to attach it to your assemblage. You can do this by attaching the back of the doll to something solid and three-dimensional, such as a small wooden block, and gluing the piece into your assemblage. The wooden block provides stability, but it can be bulky, cumbersome, and space-consuming. Another option is to attach your paper doll with a small, lightweight paper easel.

Creating an Easel Stand

1 **To begin, cut a strip of cardstock** and fold it into a straight-sided triangle. Your easel should be at least 1" (2.5 cm) tall to securely prop up your paper doll. You can use a taller easel if you have enough space in the back of your paper doll to conceal it.

2 **Adhere the straight side of the triangle** to the back of your doll. Glue the short side, the bottom, to the assemblage; the third, slanted side should keep your doll standing straight. If the edges of your easel stick out from the sides of your paper doll after being adhered, trim them with small scissors.

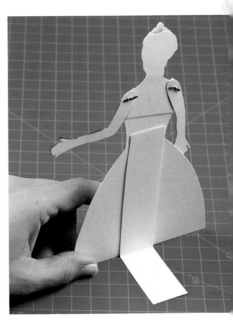

Creating an L-tab

To create an L-tab, cut a long, rectangular piece of cardstock slightly narrower than the width of the paper doll. Fold the rectangle in half widthwise and adhere one half to the paper doll and the other half to the assemblage.

Paper Dolls

Artist: Julie Molina

MARIE ANTOINETTE IN THE CASTLE DINING ROOM

RAPUNZEL IN THE CASTLE ATTIC

Artist: Paula Dion

Artist: Julie Molina

BORED DANCERS IN THE WONDERLAND HOUSE MUSIC BOX ROOM

Marie Antoinette, Castle Dining Room
Patterned scrapbook paper, with a little ink shading, was used to create this doll's queenly 'do. Patterned scrapbook paper, stamped with a pattern, was also used to create a layered dress fit for a princess.

Rapunzel, Castle Attic
This paper doll's head is covered with a princess cone and topped with a Rapunzel-like ponytail of real hair.

Gina and Jack: The Music Box Dancers, Wonderland House Music Box Room
For the Wonderland House's music box room, the artist chose to hand-draw her paper dolls—two music box dancers, bored and waiting for someone to come and wind them up. She made pencil drawings, then scanned them and used image-processing software to darken the pencil lines. The images were printed and then colored with Caran D'Ache water-soluble crayons.

NEWLYWEDS FRED AND MYRNA IN THE HOTEL'S HONEYMOON SUITE

Artist: Tally Oliveau

Artist: Paula Dion

THREE LITTLE PIGGIES IN THE WONDERLAND HOUSE

Artist: Theresa Martin

THE FEATHERLY FAMILY IN THE TREE HOUSE KITCHEN

Newlyweds, Hotel Honeymoon Suite

Newlyweds from another era embrace in the Hotel's Honeymoon Suite. A puff of white lace was attached to the bottom half of the woman to create a beautiful, three-dimensional wedding dress. This technique also serves to cover the fact that the man in the image has no legs.

Featherly Family, Tree House Kitchen

In the Tree House kitchen, a family of bird people invites us to tea. To create the little bird people, the artist scanned vintage heads and bird bodies, and, with image-processing software, digitally cut out the heads and put them onto bird bodies. The hybrid bird people were printed onto cardstock and cut out.

The Three Little Pigs Wonderland House

For the Wonderland House, the artist cut out the Three Little Piggy heads and attached them to the bodies of little girls from a vintage image collage sheet. She then added a small but important detail—a piece of fabric—to one of the girl's hands. This little piggy is holding onto her blanky, which protects her from nightmares of the big bad wolf.

Merpeople, Under the Sea House

Many of the dolls for the Under the Sea House sport mermaid tails. Some of the artists used vintage images of fish tails; others cut patterned paper into freeform shapes, to give the mermaids different swimming and lounging positions. To ensure that the top and bottom halves of the mermaids join neatly, use the tracing-paper method described on page 70.

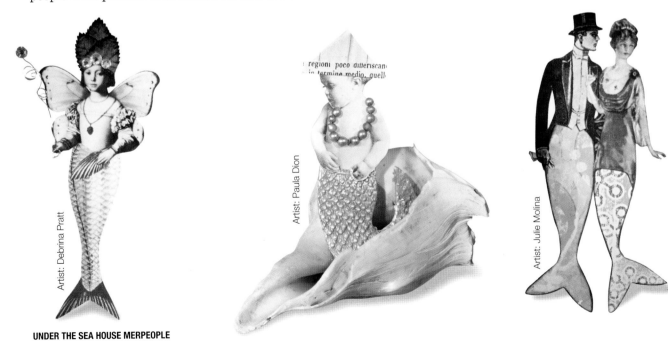

Artist: Debrina Pratt

Artist: Paula Dion

Artist: Julie Molina

UNDER THE SEA HOUSE MERPEOPLE

Beyond Paper

THE BENEFITS OF PAPER are its light weight and its ability to be manipulated and altered in various ways. But don't feel you need to restrict yourself to dolls and other figures made from paper. Figures in your assemblage can be created out of just about anything: fabric, porcelain, metal, wood. You can also create hybrid figures that are part paper and part metal.

If you want to ease into making dolls from materials other than paper, start with a "transitional" doll—a figure that's partly paper and partly another material. For example, you might make the doll's head, arms, and legs from paper and construct the torso from another material—watch parts, perhaps. You might make a face or head from stamped and baked polymer clay. A cache of vintage porcelain dolls can make their way into your assemblage. Altered and painted plastic doll heads and other parts work well, too. Don't restrict yourself to one medium—mix them up; use what you're drawn to, what speaks to you, and, of course, what you've been saving for that "special project."

Paper Alternatives

- clay (paper and polymer)—use face molds to create polymer clay faces and heads, or make individual body parts, such as limbs, and attach them with wire or jump rings, to create a completely articulated doll
- fabric—make some or all of the clothes for your doll with fabric, or sew a soft fabric doll with an embroidered face
- wood—try clothespins, spools, and blank wooden dolls found on the Internet
- glass—glass bottles make wonderful full skirts or a base for an art doll
- metal—make a hoop skirt from wire and attach it to the torso of a vintage doll
- papier mâché—bend a pipe cleaner into a doll shape and cover it with papier mâché
- porcelain and plastic dolls—alter them with paint, decoupage, and embellishments

THE JACK-IN-THE-BOX CLOWNS IN THE CIRCUS HOUSE ATTIC ARE TRANSITIONAL DOLLS.

Artist: Theresa Martin

Creating a Jack-in-the-Box Clown

The jack-in-the-box clowns combine paper, wire, and wooden blocks to create an unusual type of paper doll.

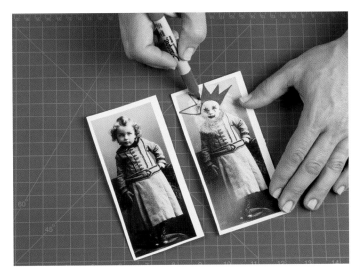

Materials

- image from a vintage collage sheet
- gesso
- paint
- wire
- pen or dowel
- wood blocks
- awl, pliers, and scissors
- adhesive

1 **Begin by choosing a child's image** from a vintage collage sheet or cabinet card. For this doll, we only need the head and neck portion of the image. To create the jack-in-the-box clown face, first paint over the face with a thin layer of gesso, making sure the face remains visible through the paint when it dries. Do not paint over the eyes.

2 **When the gesso is dry,** paint the face. Give the clown red lips, eye makeup, and any kind of hair or hat that strikes your fancy. Use the expression on the face of the child to make your clown happy, sad—or even scary!

3 **For the spring,** wrap a thin piece of wire several times around a pen or dowel and carefully slide it off. Cut the wire, being sure to leave a tail about ½" (1.3 cm) long at each end. The tails will serve as attachment sites for the face and the wood-block base. (For more about creating a wire spring, see chapter 4, page 57.)

4 **Paint the wood block** to match the colors of the room. When dry, use an awl to make a small hole in the top of the block. Attach one end of the spring to the block by inserting it into the hole, and add a drop of strong adhesive, such as E-6000, to secure the spring. When the glue is dry, cut out the clown face, leaving about 1" (2.5 cm) of paper beneath the face to slide into the spring, and secure the face to the spring with glue.

Moveable Parts

DO YOU WANT TO GIVE your paper dolls moving parts? It's easy to create articulated arms, legs, and other moveable parts with an awl or small paper punch and brads. Be sure, when creating and cutting apart your paper doll, to leave enough room on the limbs to attach them to the body of your doll.

Attaching Moveable Parts

To attach moving parts to paper dolls, first make a small hole into the doll body and the limb. Place the limb to be connected on top of the body where the joint would fall, and use an awl, paper piercer, or small punch to make a hole through both pieces. Attach the limb by inserting a brad through the hole and spreading open the ends to lay flat against the back of the doll. Repeat the process with the other limbs. You can also attach limbs with eyelets, available in the scrapbooking section of most craft stores. Be careful not to squeeze the eyelet too tightly when setting it—you want to allow enough ease for the limb to move without ripping.

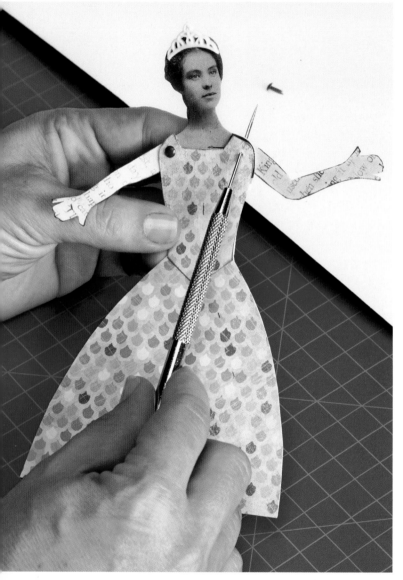

USE AN AWL, PAPER PIERCER, OR SMALL HOLE PUNCH TO POKE HOLES THROUGH THE DOLL AND LIMBS.

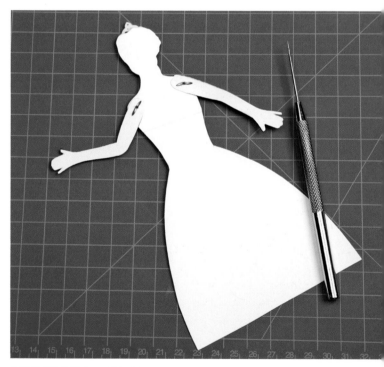

ATTACH THE ARMS WITH BRADS OR EYELETS.

Don't Forget the Pets

Artist: Paula Dion

HANGING OUT IN THE TREE HOUSE BATHROOM

Artist: Theresa Martin

A DRAGON LURKS IN THE CASTLE LIVING ROOM

No house is truly complete without a pet. But don't feel you have to limit them to dogs, cats, and fish. Our dollhouse assemblage included trike-riding monkeys, ball-balancing elephants, frog princes, bats in the belfry, and even bird TV stars. Just watch where you step—some of our friends are very tiny.

When planning your assemblage, don't forget to include pets. Animal images are available from many of the same sources that provide images of people: collage sheets, magazines, royalty-free publications, and, of course, photos of your own pets. You can personalize your piece even more by creating your own drawings, either by hand or electronically. Your pets can be paper dolls, polymer clay creatures you've created, or even store-bought, three-dimensional plastic toys. Choose a material for your pets that complements the look and feel of your assemblage.

Tree House Bathroom A chimp swings on a ladder in the Tree House bathroom, trying to get his little friend to give first dibs on the bath. The chimp is a store-bought plastic toy tied to a handmade ladder of tree branches and twine.

Castle Living Room A dragon lurks in the corner of the Castle living room, eyeing the goose in the princess's arms. Is the goose a prized pet for the princess, whose fate appears dark as the dragon approaches? Or is the goose an offering to the princess's pet dragon? A dragon image downloaded from an electronic source was printed onto heavy cardstock, cut out, and then glued into the assemblage.

Artist: Lisa Myers-Bulmash

DINNER IN THE WONDERLAND HOUSE KITCHEN

Wonderland House Kitchen In the Wonderland House kitchen, a lobster has been invited to dinner . . . make that *as* dinner. The artist found the plastic toy at a party store.

Found Treasures

Artist: Kelly Snelling

PORCELAIN ANGEL IN THE HOTEL'S LOST AND FOUND

Hotel Lost and Found A vintage porcelain angel struggles against her bonds in the Hotel's Lost and Found. The porcelain doll is tethered by copper wire to nails embedded in the walls and floor.

Castle Aviary This three-dimensional doll in the Castle aviary was created from real doll parts. Book text was decoupaged with gel medium onto the face of a plastic doll. Vintage porcelain doll arms were attached with string and wire to a birdcage body made from wire. A nest of bead eggs sits in the belly of the doll, and a tiny wooden chair was used to represent the legs.

Gothic House Attic A music-box mechanism, under a clear plastic casing, serves as the body of the doll in the Gothic House attic. A vintage illustration of a man's face and shoulders was attached to mat board for stability and attached to the plastic casing. Little black feet protrude from the bottom of the music box,

suggesting that the man is lying down . . . dead? A ghost? Perhaps he's the one haunting the Gothic House with all that spooky music.

Circus House Theater Room In the Circus House theater room, hot pink fabric flowers burst through a copper frame. The tiny flowers can be found in a craft store. The little frame was found at a scrapbooking store, but any small frame will do. You can embellish a photo slide frame for the same effect. The little glass elephant is a found object from a flea market and the wooden bird shape was found at a craft store and painted with a pearl green paint. A tiny rhinestone for an eye finishes it off.

A GHOST IN THE GOTHIC HOUSE ATTIC

FLYING HIGH IN THE CIRCUS HOUSE THEATER ROOM

THE CASTLE AVIARY DOLL

6 Fully Furnished

Now that the interiors and exteriors of your assemblage are done, it's time to start decorating! There are so many possibilities for furnishing and designing the inside of your assemblage, you might find it hard to know where to begin. A good starting point is your theme. Do you need a swing for a tree house room? A dining room table for a queen-size buffet in a castle? How about a frilly bed for your honeymoon suite? This chapter introduces the many ways you can create furnishings for your assemblage.

You can use a variety of furniture pieces in your assemblage: ready-made dollhouse furniture, furniture made from altered wood pieces, furniture made from found objects, or furniture that's been completely handmade.

Why make your own furniture? After all, ready-made dollhouse furniture is convenient and, sometimes, just the thing you need. But it can also be expensive, limited in selection, and, well, a little hoity-toity. Also, you might need a unique piece that's not commercially available. In our project, for example, the artists needed coffins, bunk beds for pigs, and a jungle bathtub, which were impossible to find, even online.

When you can't buy a piece, or when you want to create something special and personal, try making your dollhouse furniture yourself. There's a good chance that you'll be able to meet whatever challenge your imagination presents with a combination of handmade, found, and bought objects.

Building Your Furniture

LIKE YOUR ASSEMBLAGE, your furniture's look and style are open to interpretation. You can make it functional, representational, or a mix of both. You can opt out of using furniture entirely and just put a fountain in the center of the room. Much of the fun in building your own assemblage is in making it as personal and as creative (or strange and unusual) as you like.

As for materials, consider paper, wood, wire, found objects, and even plastic trinkets—any and all of these bits can be used to "build" the furniture for your altered dollhouse rooms.

Your furniture doesn't necessarily have to be functional or even three-dimensional—no dolls, fairies, birds, nor insects need actually sit on it.

In fact, your assemblage furniture might be just like the furniture in that "special" living room you remember from childhood—just for show. Furniture can be two-dimensional, made from paper and photos cut from magazines and catalogs or from images drawn and painted yourself.

Artist: Debrina Pratt

altered-object furniture

wire furniture

Paper Furniture

GOTHIC HOUSE LIVING ROOM SOFA AND HALL TABLE

A REGAL SOFA IN THE CASTLE LIVING ROOM

SQUID TABLE LEGS IN THE UNDER THE SEA HOUSE DINING ROOM

PLAYING GAMES IN THE UNDER THE SEA HOUSE CASINO ATTIC

Gothic House Living Room

The sofa and hall table in the Gothic House living room are made from catalog photos. The photos were adhered to cardstock for stability, and then the pieces were attached to the assemblage with an L-tab (see Chapter 5, page 71) to give them dimension.

Castle Living Room

The regal-looking sofa in the Castle living room is another example of catalog-photo furniture. The side table is constructed from a wine cork and paper table top.

Under the Sea House Dining Room

For the Under the Sea House dining room, the table was made from decorative paper, which was scored and folded. The furniture legs are paper printouts of blue squid. They're doing a nice job of holding up the table while still keeping an eye on that little undersea princess.

Under the Sea House Casino Attic

The casino attic in the Under the Sea House includes gaming tables and a roulette wheel, all made from paper! Real dice serve as stools.

Wood Furniture

For a traditional furniture style, look in craft stores for inexpensive miniature wood furniture. This furniture is usually unfinished and available in separate pieces, allowing you to make your own unique combinations. Although it's ready-made, it can be personalized with paint or by distressing it for an antique look. Adding custom touches to ready-made pieces makes them your own and enhances them with your own sense of style and color.

To build your own wooden furniture, consider using wood beads and the pre-cut balsa-wood shapes available in craft stores. Small wooden disks glued to wooden spools or other cylindrical pieces make seats or a small table. Glue or nail three or four rectangular pieces of wood to the wall of your assemblage and you have instant shelves. Create a bench by using a rectangular block as the base and a bit of miniature wooden fencing as the back rest. If you can't find ready-made wooden fencing, use halved craft sticks. "Stain" them with a little watered-down brown paint, and then sand them lightly after the paint dries, to "age" them.

Castle Dining Room
Heart-shaped wood pieces attached to wood ovals were set atop wooden spools to create chairs in the Castle dining room. Pink paper bonbon cups were used for the chair skirts. The table is made from pre-cut balsa wood, which was painted and stamped. The table base is a wood block adorned with a wooden fleur-de-lis, to give it that royal flair.

Circus House Dining Room
Painted wooden pieces from a craft store form the legs for the Circus House dining room table. Gold German scrap makes a lacy table skirt.

Heartbreak Hotel Room
For the Hotel's Heartbreak Hotel Room, the artist used traditional dollhouse furniture, including a nightstand to hold a mini telephone and lamp. She found the items online.

TRADITIONAL FURNITURE IN THE HEARTBREAK HOTEL ROOM

Under the Sea House Bedrooms

Wooden pieces and other found objects were used to make creative furniture pieces for the mermaid bedrooms in the Under the Sea House. In one bedroom, a wooden block was painted and rubber-stamped to become a dresser, with small wooden pieces glued to the bottom for the legs. In another bedroom, a small mirror was encrusted with small shells; it sits atop a wooden block, which was covered with tulle fabric to serve as a vanity table. A large shell is used as the mermaid's bed.

Artist: Debrina Pratt

THE MERMAID BEDROOMS IN THE UNDER THE SEA HOUSE

Artist: Paula Dion

Artist: Paula Dion

Wonderland House Bedroom Rustic

twigs were put together to create a triple bunk bed for the three little pigs in the Wonderland House bedroom. A miniature chest of drawers from a craft store was painted by the artist in bright colors.

BUNK BEDS FOR THE THREE LITTLE PIGS IN THE WONDERLAND HOUSE BEDROOM

Wire

Wire can also be used for making furniture in your assemblage. Using wire wrapping, you can make a variety of pieces, from chairs and lamps to birdcages, with a few twists and turns.

THE FLOOR LAMP IN THE TREE HOUSE LIVING ROOM WAS MADE FROM WIRE, A TINY TWINKLE LIGHT BULB, AND A PAPER FLOWER.

Artist: Debrina Pratt

Making a Wire Lamp

Materials

◆ 20-gauge wire

◆ needle-nose pliers

◆ round-nose pliers

◆ wooden dowel or thick marker

◆ spare bulb from a string of Christmas lights

◆ silk or paper flower

◆ adhesive, such as thick tacky glue or gel medium

◆ off-white or antique white craft paint

1 **To make the lamp stand,** curve the wire into decorative swirls using your round-nose pliers. Curl a large arc at one end to serve as the neck of the lamp.

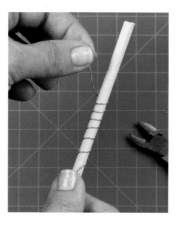

2 **Wrap the bottom end of the wire** two or three times around a dowel or thick marker, pull it off, and bend it flat, creating a base.

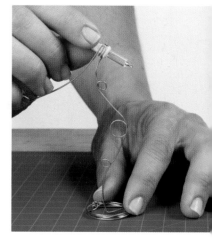

3 **Wrap the top end of the wire** around the tiny light bulb and secure it with a strong adhesive, such as thick tacky glue or gel medium.

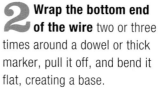

4 **Paint the wire antique white,** if desired. When dry, remove the center of a silk or paper flower and slide it over the light bulb to create the shade. Adhere it with tacky glue or gel medium.

Tip

The length of your wire is determined by how tall you want your lamp to be and how many decorative loops it will have. If you don't know how much wire you'll need, work directly off the spool, cutting off the end of the wire only when you've finished your piece of furniture. We used 12"–18" (30.5–45.7 cm) of wire for this example.

Found Objects

When you're thinking creatively, you can find many uses for found objects and items you've purchased for another purpose. A jar becomes a table base. A birdcage becomes a swing. A gourd becomes a bathtub, and a wine cork becomes a chair. With a little practice, you'll be seeing alternative uses for all sorts of found objects.

Artist: Debrina Pratt

Ways with Found Objects

◆ Carve a chunk from a wine cork with a craft knife to form an L-shaped chair. Adhere it directly to the floor, or set it into a plastic or metal bottle-cap base.

◆ Create a swing by wrapping wire around each end of a vintage harmonica and suspending it from the ceiling.

◆ Adhere watch parts, cogs, and gears in a loose formation to the back wall of your assemblage, to provide the illusion of working "machinery."

◆ Use old watch faces and parts to add a vintage, Steampunk look to a room. Suspend them with wire from the ceiling or adhere them to the floor or walls. (Steampunk is a stylistic genre of art in which natural and industrial objects are combined in fantastical and unlikely ways.)

◆ Use a watch face as a miniature wall clock.

◆ Create a glass-topped table, window, or bubble from an old optometrist's lens.

Optometrist's Lens Window

To create a window, drill or cut a hole into the wall of your assemblage box slightly smaller than the size of the lens. You want the hole to be slightly smaller to give the lens something to adhere to. Place the lens over the hole and adhere it to the inside or outside of the wall (depending on your preference) with a thick tacky glue. If your lens has a handle, drill a small hole through the handle and nail the lens by the handle to your assemblage. Using a nail that is thinner than the hole in the handle allows your lens to swing freely on the nail, adding movement and interest to your piece. To give the hole a finished look, cover any rough edges with decorative paper. You can also add a little flair by surrounding the window or covering any glue or mistakes with stones, shells, or small, flat-sided beads.

Artist: Theresa Martin

Found Objects

Artist: Debrina Pratt

ELEGANT CHAIRS AND A FANCY TABLE IN THE WONDERLAND HOUSE TEA ROOM

Artist: Lisa Myers-Bulmash

WONDERLAND HOUSE KITCHEN CHAIRS

Artist: Paula Dion

JUNGLE JANE'S BATH IN THE TREE HOUSE JUNGLE BATHROOM

Artist: Paula Dion

FURNISHINGS IN THE GOTHIC HOUSE LIVING AND DINING ROOMS

Wonderland House Kitchen The chairs in the Wonderland House kitchen are carved from wine corks.

Wonderland House Tea Room For the Wonderland House tea room, wire was wrapped into the forms of two very fancy chairs and painted antique white. The seats are topped with fabric-covered buttons, and small beads form the "feet." The beautiful table base was created from a small glass jar and a bottle cap.

Tree House Jungle Bathroom In the Tree House jungle bathroom, the bottom half of a gourd, which was cut with a craft knife, serves as an inviting bathtub for Jungle Jane—she's got her leopard-print washcloth all ready to go. The bathtub is filled with Ultra Thick Embossing Powder, which was mixed with glitter, melted, and poured into the gourd, in which it hardened to look like sparkling water.

Gothic House The furniture in the Gothic House living room was made from wooden spools and blocks. The table base in the dining room was made from miniature skulls.

Artist: Tally Oliveau

TREASURE IN THE UNDER THE SEA HOUSE TREASURE ROOM

Under the Sea House Treasure Room

A found toy treasure chest was used in the Under the Sea House Treasure Room. It was painted and distressed to give it a realistic look.

Hotel Branches, a lace-covered wood block, and lace trim come together to form the canopy bed in the Hotel's Honeymoon Suite. The bed in the Hotel spa (below) was created from fabric-covered cotton batting, held in place by stapling fabric to the underside of each cardboard piece and then attaching the pieces to the sides of a wooden block.

Artist: Tally Oliveau

THE HOTEL'S HONEYMOON SUITE CANOPY BED

Artist: Lisa Myers-Bulmash

THE HOTEL SPA BED

Found-Object Furniture in the Wonderland House Attic

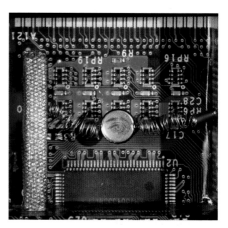

Artist: Tally Oliveau

A PLASTIC TOY, ALTERED WITH PAINT AND ELECTRICAL PARTS; A PLASTIC TOY EYEBALL ON A PAINTED WEDDING CAKE PEDESTAL; A PLAIN WOOD BLOCK BECOMES AN ELECTRICAL CONDUIT FOR AN ALL-SEEING EYE.

Furniture from Scratch

Whether it's a size issue or you just can't find what you're looking for, sometimes the only option is to make a piece of furniture from scratch. To start construction, gather together a craft knife, a straight edge, and some mat board, then look for a template, which will make the process easier. Use the template to mark your cutting lines. Once your shape is cut out, draw on it, paper it, or paint it.

Mat board is versatile and works well for making table tops, chests of drawers (you'll need to draw on the drawers and add beads for drawer pulls), window frames, doors, and many other three-dimensional creations—even coffins.

THE CUSTOM-MADE COFFIN WAS CUT FROM MAT BOARD, GLUED TOGETHER WITH DIMENSIONAL ADHESIVE, AND THEN PAINTED AND EMBELLISHED.

The Red Chairs

The artist who created these rooms used a set of bright-red, miniature metal chairs found at a local flea market to create a running style marker throughout all her rooms. She used at least one red chair in all of her room assemblages, making each room easily identifiable as her work. The red chairs add a pop of bright color and are perfect places for the paper dolls to sit when their little paper feet get tired.

THREE RED CHAIRS PROVIDE COLOR AND INTEREST TO THE VINTAGE-STYLE, MUTED TONES OF THE HOTEL ATTIC; IS THE RED CHAIR A SIGN OF DANGER? IT DRAWS THE EYE TO THE CORNER OF THE ROOM IN WHICH THE DRAGON LURKS. PERHAPS THE PRINCESS HAD BETTER NOT SIT DOWN. THE CHAIR COLOR IS REFLECTED IN OTHER PARTS OF THE ROOM, BY THE CRAB, THE CORAL, AND THE RED STARS. THE COLOR IS A BEAUTIFUL CONTRAST TO THE UNDERSEA BLUES.

Artist: Theresa Martin

7 Embellishments

By now, your assemblage is really coming together. The paint or wallpaper is up, the floors are done, the windows installed, and most of your furniture is built. You've arrived at one of the best parts of designing your assemblage: embellishing it with fabric and accessories. Because you are working on a small scale, your fabric elements can consist of myriad items: ribbon, scraps of lace, bits of trim. Even leftover fabric scraps can add a touch of softness and realism to your assemblage.

The crystal ball makes the perfect accessory for a gypsy fortune teller.

Jewelry findings embellish the windows as wind chimes.

A skirted table with fabric embellishments adds to the ambiance.

Artist: Julie Molina

Fabric-ation

IF YOU'VE BEEN SAVING SMALL BITS OF FABRIC that you love, now is the time to put them to work. A vintage piece of lace can become the trim of a canopy bed. A vintage handkerchief, found at a flea market, might become a tablecloth. A ribbon from a favorite gift is the perfect trim for a princess's dress. Leftover fabric makes wonderful wall tapestries, curtains, and bedspreads. You can even cut up old stuffed animals to make beanbag chairs, couches, or rugs.

If you don't have a drawer or box full of fabric remnants, visit a craft or fabric store—many sell remnant packs that are perfect for this use. Any small bit of fabric can make a big statement. This is the time to use the good stuff: Instead of letting it sit in a drawer, use it to create something beautiful to be displayed and admired.

IN THE GOTHIC HOUSE GYPSY DEN, THE FORTUNE TELLER'S TABLE HIDES MANY SECRETS UNDER ITS SKIRT, MADE FROM INDIAN SARI FABRIC.

Creating a Skirted Table

To create the table, start by printing an image of a mandala from your computer and cutting it out. The mandala will become a decorative table top. You can make your own unique mandala and kaleidoscope images at www.krazydad.com/kaleido/

Materials

- mat or foam board for the table top
- printed mandala or other table-top design
- pins
- craft knife
- wooden or plastic spool for the table base
- tacky glue or gel medium
- fabric for the table skirt
- masking tape
- German scrap or other embellishments

1 Use the cut-out mandala image to trace a circle of the same size onto a piece of foam or mat board. Cut out the circle with a craft knife. This is the table top.

2 Glue the table top to a wooden or plastic spool table base.

3 Measure the circumference of the table (for the fabric length) and the distance from the edge of the table to the floor (for the fabric width) and cut a strip of fabric to size.

4 Using tacky glue or gel medium, adhere the fabric around the edge of the foam table top. Use straight pins to keep the fabric in place while your glue dries. Push the pins into the foam, being careful to keep them straight so they don't pierce through the table top. The pins can be pushed in all the way and left in place or removed when the glue has dried.

5 Now glue the cut mandala to the top of the table. Adhere a piece of German scrap around the table to cover any unfinished fabric edges or pins left in place. Tip: Insert another pin where the edges of the German scrap meet, to ensure that they lay flat and do not come undone. Once the glue is dry, you can add other adornments to your table. In this gypsy's room, a

glass marble was used for the crystal ball, small glass bottles filled with beads represent the "potions," and vintage glass buttons become little dishes and containers for spell ingredients.

Tip A finished edge on the table skirt can be easily and quickly achieved by "hemming" the fabric on the underside with masking or other tape. No sewing is required!

Fabrics

Artist: Theresa Martin

THE HOTEL PENTHOUSE CURTAINS AND BED

Artist: Paula Dion

THE HEARTBREAK HOTEL ROOM BEDDING

Hotel Penthouse Satin fabric was used to create the curtains in the main room of the Hotel penthouse. A wide, ornate ribbon was used for a valance. The ribbon is backed by heavy cardstock to give it more stability and support. The same ornate ribbon from the curtains was fitted around the bed to give it the look of a bed skirt and unify the pieces in the room. Another option is to cover a child's wooden block or a small gift box in a little cotton batting and some satin fabric, held in place with fabric glue or white glue. If you're good with a needle and thread, you can sew the fabric and ribbon onto the box.

Castle Attic Various patterns and textures of fabric were layered to create a realistic and cozy-looking bed in the Castle attic. The canopy is another bit of fabric with lovely scalloped edges. The fabric was glued to the top of a small box lid to provide stability and a canopy shape. A strip of decorative paper, resembling a baroque tapestry, finishes off the canopy.

Heartbreak Hotel Room Elvis invites you into the Hotel's Heartbreak Hotel Room to try out the pretty pink bed with ruffled skirt and hand-sewn, heart-shaped pillows.

THE CASTLE ATTIC BEDDING

Artist: Paula Dion

(Continued, page 98)

Castle Bedroom The Castle bedroom and attic feature hand-sewn pillows and bedding adorned with wonderful little accents, such as silk flowers and trim, that reflect the posh bedding of a princess. In the bedroom, a scrap of velvet fabric was glued to a round papier mâché box and stuffed with a small amount of cotton batting. A ruffled piece of matching trim was added around the edge of the bed, turning the bottom of the velvet fabric into a beautiful bed skirt. Gold ribbon hides the seam between the batting and the bed skirt.

Artist: Debrina Pratt

THE CASTLE BEDROOM BEDDING

All the Trimmings

BEADS, BUTTONS, and other small bits of metal, trim, and found objects can be given new life within the miniature world of your assemblage.

Beads, Buttons, and Bits

As an artist or crafter, you probably have a stash of beads, buttons, and found objects in drawers or jars. Your assemblage is the perfect excuse to use them. Here are some ideas:

◆ A handful of imitation pearls or clear plastic beads make great bubbles in a bubble bath. Use a small teacup or dipping dish for the tub. Fill it with glue or clear resin, add your beads—instant bubble bath.

◆ A lone, dangly earring can become a chandelier. Straighten out the hook, drill a small hole through your box, poke the end of the earring wire through, and bend it flat against the outside of the box. Adhere the wire with strong tape.

◆ Use bead caps, available from bead shops and craft stores, as fancy bowls. Fill your bowls with tiny beads to represent fruit, candies, or petit fours.

◆ Cone-shaped bead caps make perfect little vases for tiny flowers. Thread the flowers through the bead caps until you have a nice arrangement. Cut off the excess wire and dab some glue at the bottom of the cone to hold the flowers in place. Then glue the cone of flowers to a table or a wall.

◆ Create a wall sconce by adhering a miniature Christmas light to the inside of a cone-shaped bead cap. Use a strong glue, such as E-6000, when working with metals, to provide a firmer hold.

Trimmings

Artist: Lisa Myers-Bulmash

RIPPLING RIBBON IN THE UNDER THE SEA HOUSE BUBBLE ROOM

Under the Sea House Bubble Room

Ribbon in shades of blue and green, representing water, ripple above the mermaid's head in the Under the Sea House Bubble Room. The ribbon can be glued to the ceiling with a tacky glue or gel medium or even tacked on with a staple gun.

Wonderland House Bedroom In the
little pigs' bedroom of the Wonderland House, the artist sewed custom pillows and used remnants of lace in the bunk beds. The lace adds a canopy to this sweet little room.

Artist: Paula Dion

VINTAGE LACE TRIM IN THE WONDERLAND HOUSE LITTLE PIGS' BEDROOM

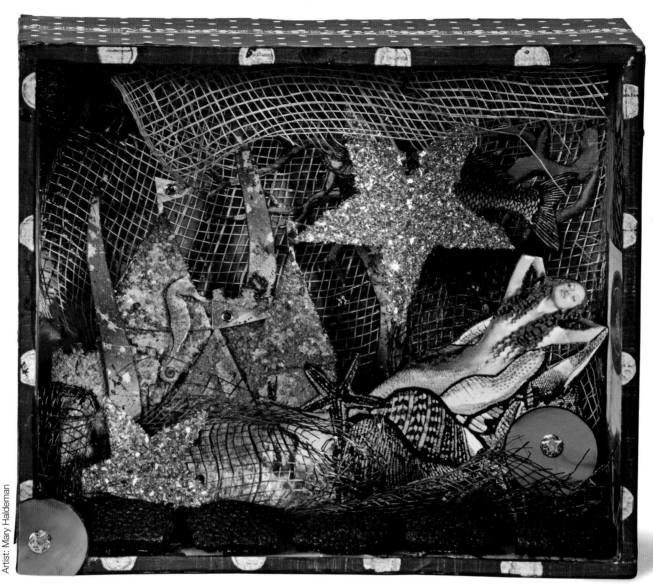

Artist: Mary Haldeman

NETTING IN THE UNDER THE SEA HOUSE BEDROOM

Artist: Debrina Pratt

JINGLE BELLS IN THE CIRCUS HOUSE KITCHEN

Under the Sea House Bedroom

Netting was used to create texture in the Under the Sea House bedroom. Perhaps the mermaid is using a fisherman's net as a hammock.

Circus House Kitchen
A strip of gold fabric trim across the top of the Circus House kitchen finishes it off nicely and provides a place to hang tiny jingle bells. The little clowns drink their coffee from mugs made from silver necklace beads. Colorful wooden beads stacked and glued with white glue form the table legs. One of the most interesting elements of the room is the tiny, vintage flea-market harmonica, acting as the monkey's swing.

Circus House Theater Room

Circus House Theater Room A hand-drawn sun and a fancy toothpick form the mask of this high-flying doll in the Circus House theater room. The acrobat's wild hair is a bit of fabric trim, glued around the head, her feet are adorned with plastic star beads, and she swings from a large key ring, which has been wrapped with multicolored knitting yarn. Her fellow acrobats are little plastic ballerinas that are usually found perched on cupcakes. They were painted gold and suspended with wire from the ceiling.

Under the Sea House Treasure Room This Treasure Room is bursting with bits of broken jewelry, shells, beads, and pearls that represent the precious treasure that some people might be willing to die for. Looks like someone got stuck in this room some time ago. The treasure chest is a painted and distressed child's toy.

Gothic House Moon Room Found watch parts dangle from the ceiling and lie on the floor of the Gothic House Moon Room. They're metaphors for the passage of time and the phases of the moon.

Artist: Julie Molina

ACROBATICS IN THE CIRCUS HOUSE THEATER ROOM

Artist: Tally Oliveau

PRECIOUS "JEWELS" IN THE UNDER THE SEA HOUSE TREASURE ROOM

Artist: Theresa Martin

TIME PASSING IN THE GOTHIC HOUSE MOON ROOM.

Materials from Mother Nature

Although craft stores are brimming with items representing natural elements, why not go the natural route and collect real elements from nature for your assemblage? The woods, the beach, and your own backyard are great places to look for natural materials. Real flowers and leaves wilt, but twigs, stones, and seashells stand the test of time. Other natural objects to consider are nut shells, dried seed pods and seeds, pine cones, dried moss, feathers, pieces of bark, wooden skewers, and sea glass. Choose lightweight items, so you don't overburden your assemblage.

A seashell makes the perfect headboard for a tiny mermaid's bed. A piece cut from a thick branch forms a beautiful table top. Adhere a branch across the top of your room and hang a curtain from it, to create a fairy stage. Remove the back "wall" of your assemblage encasement and hang a swing from the branch using natural twine.

To create the look of a tree growing in and out of the walls of your assemblage, cut up a twisted, curvy branch and glue the pieces to the walls and ceiling. Have the pieces continue around the room, as if you had built your room around it.

Faking Mother Nature

If you're not especially keen on nature, you can find lots of elements to fake it in craft stores: seashells, stones, and sea glass by the bagful; beads, feathers, and faux birds; plastic, paper, and silk flowers and foliage. A silk flower can double as a beautiful chair or bed. Fabric or paper leaves and flowers lining the floor of a room form a luxurious "carpet." Hang silk or glass leaf beads to twigs and add plastic flower blossoms or colorful beads to represent fruit.

Natural and Faux Natural Elements

Tree House Attic Moss can be used to hide a multitude of sins. It can cover up globs of glue and uneven cutting or fill in too much negative space. It adds a lovely, three-dimensional touch and really brings the outside in.

Wonderland House Bedroom In the Wonderland House bedroom, Alice is surrounded by a beautiful array of paper foliage that was printed from commercially available clip art. Foliage can also be rubber stamped or drawn onto heavy cardstock and cut out. Support paper foliage as you would a paper doll, and layer various foliage sizes and heights to add depth.

Castle Aviary The artist brought the outside in by creating a tree in the Castle aviary from a real branch. Ornamenting the tree are birdcages cut from paper and sandwiched between sheets of mica. A hole was punched into the mica and a grommet attached, to hang the cages from wrapped wire hooks. A final touch is the lovely blue ribbon not quite wrapped around the bottom of the tree. The ribbon not only covers the glue and possible uneven cut of the branch, it also provides a great pop of color and gives the illusion of movement on a windy day.

THE MOSSY TREE HOUSE ATTIC

Artist: Gale Blair

Artist: Theresa Martin

PAPER FOLIAGE IN THE WONDERLAND HOUSE BEDROOM

Artist: Deryn Mentock

THE CASTLE AVIARY TREE

8 Thinking Outside the Box

"Thinking outside the box" is a phrase that has become overused in the last few years, but, in this chapter we mean it literally and figuratively. Now that you have a vision for your assemblage, you'll want to start thinking about other things you can do to make it even more interesting, such as creating additional artwork, or extending your artwork, beyond the interior of the box to its exterior. A first step might be to collage the box exterior, then add paper dolls or other embellishments. This is where we start thinking outside the box.

Embellishing the Box Exterior

A GOOD WAY TO START working on the outside of your assemblage box is by embellishing it. Exterior embellishments should match and continue the theme, mood, and message of your assemblage interiors. They can include papers and images that have been adhered flat against the outside of the box or three-dimensional materials that protrude from or into your assemblage. For our project, for example, paper dolls "walked" around the outside of the rooms. Many artists also attached metal and wood frames to their exteriors to further embellish their cutouts, a good example of not allowing the walls of the assemblage to confine you.

Here are some tips for embellishing the exterior of your assemblage:

◆ Embellish the exterior in paint colors and images that fit your theme. For example, the exterior of the Gothic House was painted black, and the Under the Sea House was painted in blues and greens.

◆ Extend your theme beyond the assemblage interior. The exteriors of the Castle rooms, for example, were collaged to resemble cobblestones. Papers were cut into window moldings. Images attached to the assemblage exteriors extend the interior activity to the outside.

◆ Add elements—tree branches, for example—that extend from the interior to the exterior and vice versa.

◆ Create interest and activity by introducing paper dolls or figures to the outside of your assemblage walls.

◆ Frame window and door cutouts on both the interior and exterior of the assemblage.

◆ Add unusual box shapes or sizes to create additional interest and space to your assemblage. What accessory spaces (castle rotundas, hotel elevators) might transform your assemblage from ordinary to eye-catching?

What's Going on Outside?

IN ADDITION TO EMBELLISHING THE EXTERIOR of your
assemblage, introduce relevant activities that take place outside of the rooms
and that fit your theme or concept. Perhaps tropical leaves cover the exterior
of the jungle safari-room box. Are those creepy insects crawling around
outside? Let tree branches, doll arms and legs, wrapped and coiled wire, or
even bird wings extend beyond the confines of your assemblage walls. These
embellishments can be glued on or attached to the box with cold joins. Use a
drill or an awl to make a small hole through the assemblage wall and bolt or
nail down those extensions.

Attach more boxes for adjacent rooms.

Use the top of the box as another room.

Artist: Theresa Martin

Exterior Embellishments

A PATIO ATOP THE HOTEL ATTIC

Artist: Theresa Martin

Hotel Honeymoon Suite Windows with decorative moldings frame words relating to the Honeymoon Suite theme on the inside of the assemblage. The words—trust, love, and compromise—are masked slightly by the netting in the windows, conveying the idea that these concepts are not always clear to partners in a long-term successful marriage or relationship.

Hotel Attic The Hotel attic uses the exterior as additional space for rooms. The roof of the penthouse, for example, is also the floor of the patio above. Two smaller-size boxes attached to the side of the assemblage form an additional "room" and an elevator.

Wonderland House Dining Room For the Wonderland house dining room, the artist continued the dining room theme by attaching a large spoon to the exterior. She also added a two-dimensional paper doll and other embellishments to suit the theme of her interior.

Tree House For the Tree House nesting room, the artist extended the branch from the interior to the exterior of the assemblage. Another artist extends a sign from the exterior wall of the Tree House living room, more elements reaching out.

A SPOON SAYS "DINNER" ON THE EXTERIOR
OF THE WONDERLAND HOUSE DINING ROOM.

EXTERIOR WINDOW TREATMENTS ON THE HOTEL'S HONEYMOON SUITE

THE TREE HOUSE LIVING ROOM EXTENDS A SIGN.

BRANCHING OUT IN THE TREE HOUSE NESTING ROOM

Castle Attic A cylindrical box, formerly a wine-bottle gift box, added to the side of the Castle attic gives this assemblage character. Every storybook castle has rotundas and turrets, presumably with some beautiful princess locked away inside. The cylinder is topped with a realistic looking roof, made from a rolled and painted strip of corrugated paper.

Gothic House Attic The artist added a typical household element to the Gothic House attic—a chimney. Of course, this is no ordinary chimney; it was created with miniature wood fencing, found at a craft store, and a rubber-stamped image.

Wonderland House Attic The exterior of the Wonderland House Attic suggests a face, so the artists extended a cone from the center for its nose.

Wonderland House Bedroom The three little pigs hide from the big bad wolf, waiting at the window of the Wonderland House bedroom.

Circus House Attic A metal monkey rides a trike on the roof of the Circus House attic. The monkey fits the theme of the assemblage perfectly, conjuring up images of circus animals and trapeze acts, all in one small piece. The figurine was attached by drilling holes through the attic roof and cold joining it with copper wire.

GOTHIC HOUSE ATTIC CHIMNEY

Artist: Lisa Myers-Bulmash

Artist: Paula Dion

THE CASTLE ATTIC ROTUNDA

WONDERLAND HOUSE ATTIC NOSE CONE

Artist: Tally Oliveau

A TRIKE-RIDING MONKEY ON THE
ROOF OF THE CIRCUS HOUSE ATTIC

Artist: Theresa Martin

Artist: Paula Dion

THE BIG BAD WOLF HOWLS AT THE WINDOW
OF THE WONDERLAND HOUSE BEDROOM.

9

The Gallery

The Tree House

Branches reaching tall
Hear the birds call
Come and play inside
Ponder the blue
Nesting love so true
Come and play inside.

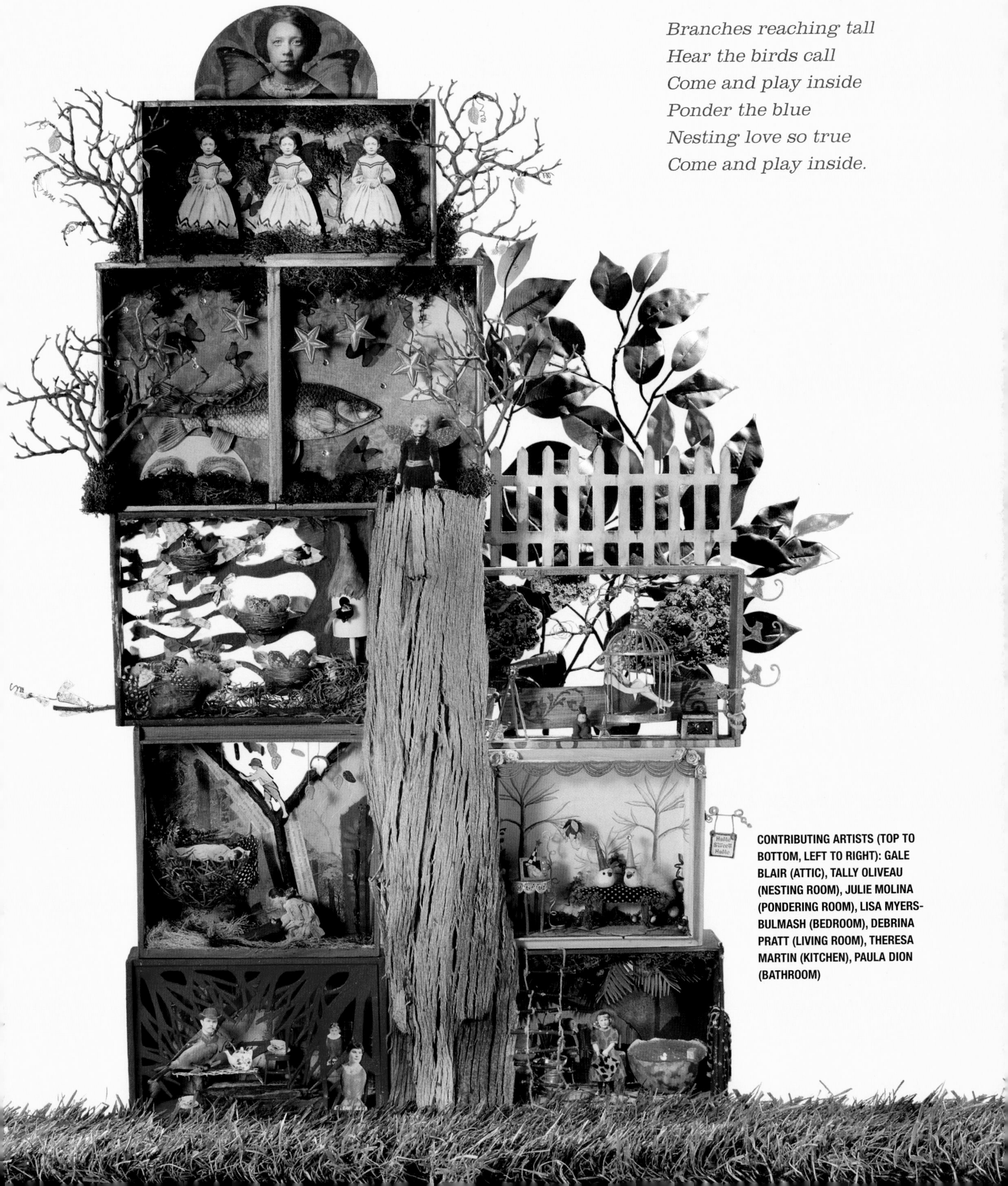

The Gothic House

The dark draws near
Bringing gothic fear
Come and play inside
Vampire's awake
While the witches flight take
Come and play inside.

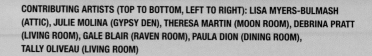

CONTRIBUTING ARTISTS (TOP TO BOTTOM, LEFT TO RIGHT): LISA MYERS-BULMASH (ATTIC), JULIE MOLINA (GYPSY DEN), THERESA MARTIN (MOON ROOM), DEBRINA PRATT (LIVING ROOM), GALE BLAIR (RAVEN ROOM), PAULA DION (DINING ROOM), TALLY OLIVEAU (LIVING ROOM)

The Castle

Castle rare
Maiden fair
Come and play inside
Dragon creep
Turret steep
Come and play inside.

ROYAL PINK

CONTRIBUTING ARTISTS (TOP TO BOTTOM, LEFT TO RIGHT): PAULA DION (ATTIC AND ROTUNDA),TALLY OLIVEAU (LIBRARY), THERESA MARTIN (LIVING ROOM), JULIE MOLINA (DINING ROOM),LISA MYERS-BULMASH (DUNGEON), DEBRINA PRATT (BEDROOM), DERYN MENTOCK (AVIARY)

The Under the Sea House

Azure blue
Mermaid dreams can come true
Come and play inside
Spin the roulette wheel
Let's make a deal!
Come and play inside.

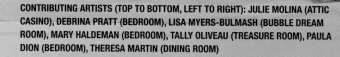

CONTRIBUTING ARTISTS (TOP TO BOTTOM, LEFT TO RIGHT): JULIE MOLINA (ATTIC CASINO), DEBRINA PRATT (BEDROOM), LISA MYERS-BULMASH (BUBBLE DREAM ROOM), MARY HALDEMAN (BEDROOM), TALLY OLIVEAU (TREASURE ROOM), PAULA DION (BEDROOM), THERESA MARTIN (DINING ROOM)

The Circus House

The circus clown
Has come to town
Come and play inside
Trapeze artist leap
Audience claps on its feet
Come and play inside.

CONTRIBUTING ARTISTS (TOP TO BOTTOM, LEFT TO RIGHT): THERESA MARTIN (ATTIC),
JULIE MOLINA (TRAPEZE ROOM), DEBRINA PRATT (DINING ROOM), TALLY OLIVEAU
(NIGHTMARE BEDROOM), PAULA DION (MAKEUP ROOM), LISA MYERS-BULMASH
(BATHROOM) LUPE PADILLA-MITCHELL (SIDESHOW ROOM)

The Hotel

Check in, check out
I'll take the suite, no doubt
Come and play inside
View the city lights
Take me to new heights
Come and play inside.

CONTRIBUTING ARTISTS (TOP TO BOTTOM, LEFT TO RIGHT): THERESA MARTIN
(PENTHOUSE SUITE), DEBRINA PRATT (LOLLIPOP GIFT SHOP), TALLY OLIVEAU
(HONEYMOON SUITE), JULIE MOLINA (LOBBY), KELLY SNELLING (LOST AND FOUND),
PAULA DION (HEARTBREAK HOTEL ROOM), LISA MYERS-BULMASH (SPA)

The Wonderland House

You know it's time
To bend your mind
Come and play inside
Alice and space await
But first, check your plate
Come and play inside.

CONTRIBUTING ARTISTS (TOP TO BOTTOM, LEFT TO RIGHT): TALLY OLIVEAU (ATTIC/MIND'S EYE), DEBRINA PRATT (TEA ROOM), THERESA MARTIN (ALICE'S BEDROOM), CARYL HOOBLER (CANDYLAND NURSERY), LISA MYERS-BULMASH (KITCHEN), JULIE MOLINA (MUSIC BOX), PAULA DION (THREE LITTLE PIGS' BEDROOM)

Appendix

COPYRIGHT-FREE VINTAGE CABINET CARD IMAGES FOR USE IN PAPER DOLL MAKING

PAPER DOLL TEMPLATE

WINDOW FRAME TEMPLATES

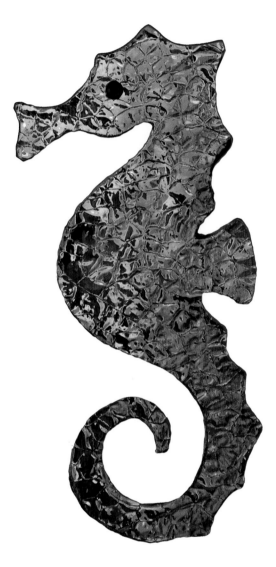

COPYRIGHT-FREE IMAGES FOR AN UNDER THE SEA THEME

IMAGES OF SHUTTERS

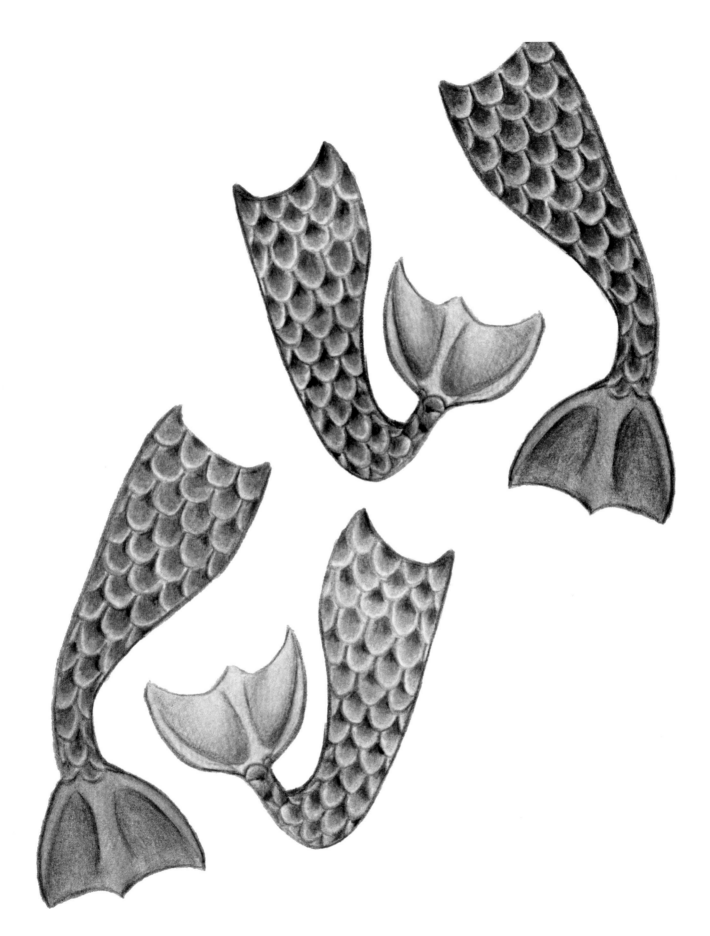

MERMAID TAILS FOR PAPER DOLLS

Resources

www.artchixstudio.com
collage sheets of vintage images for paper doll making, ephemera, and art goodies
for assemblage

www.dickblick.com
general discount art supplier

www.doverpublishing.com
copyright-free clip art books and images

www.ebay.com
online auction site – source for vintage and new goodies
search key words: ephemera, vintage letters, vintage ledger, vintage paper, cabinet cards

www.flickr.com/groups/collageimages
source for images that can be used in artwork

www.krazydad.com/kaleido
make your own kaleidoscope/mandala table top as described in Chapter 6

www.mcphee.com
funky and fun ephemera for assemblage

www.paperwhimsy.com
collage sheets of vintage images for paper doll making, ephemera, and art goodies for
assemblage

www.silvercrowcreations.com
art rubber stamps, art supplies, shrine supplies, and more

www.vintageimagemadness.com
source for digital vintage images and ephemera

Contributors

Gale Blair

hello@paperwhimsy.com
www.paperwhimsy.com

Paula Dion

pollydion@embarqmail.com

Mary Haldeman

mehaldeman@aol.com
www.picturetrail.com/maryhaldeman

Caryl Hoobler

carylsrealm@yahoo.com
http://carylsrealm.blogspot.com

Theresa Martin

info@theresamartin.com
www.theresamartin.com

Deryn Mentock

mocknet@sbcglobal.net
http://somethingsublime.typepad.com

Tally Oliveau

tally@papierstudio.com
www.papierstudio.com
www.tallyoliveau.blogspot.com

Lisa Myers-Bulmash

yolisalisa@gmail.com
www.bloggingqueen.com

Lupe Padilla-Mitchell

beyondnormalart@ymail.com
www.beyondnormalart.com

Julie Molina

julie.molina@mac.com
www.madhatstudio.com

Debrina Pratt

landofenchantment@sbcglobal.net
http://whimsicalworldoffairies.blogspot.com

Kelly Snelling

smallbird@cox.net
www.kellysnelling.etsy.com
http://soulhumming.typepad.com

About the Authors

TALLY OLIVEAU is a collage and mixed-media artist and has been widely published in *Somerset Studio* magazine, *Belle Amoire*, *Somerset Memories*, and *Somerset Home* magazines. In addition, Tally is the president of Papier Studio, a greeting card company. Her artistic cards are sold in stores all over the country. She lives and teaches in Los Angeles, California.

tally@papierstudio.com
www.papierstudio.com

JULIE MOLINA has worked as a collage and mixed-media artist since 2001. She has been published in several of Stampington's publications including *Somerset Studio* magazine and her work is included in *1000 Artist Journal Pages* by Dawn DeVries Sokol, © 2008 Quarry Books. Julie lives in Los Angeles, California.

julie.molina@mac.com
www.madhatstudio.com

Acknowledgments

TO MY BEAUTIFUL FAMILY, especially Steve, who continues to give me love, and supports my madness, all with a smile.

–Tally

I'D LIKE TO THANK MY HUSBAND and best friend, Jose, who lets me play all day long with ALMOST no complaints.

–Julie

TO MARY ANN HALL, Winnie Prentiss, Pat Price and all the amazing people at Quarry Books who appreciate our vision enough to help us make this book a reality. They guided us through this extensive process with patience and open-minded creativity.

We also want to thank the incredibly talented artists who contributed to this project, taking on this unusual endeavor with vigor and excitement for something new. It was fun, wasn't it? Finally, we want to thank all the artists out there who continue to put themselves out of their own comfort zones, using "the good stuff" every day, displaying their hearts and souls in their art for all the world to see.